Passive Income

(3 Books in 1)

John James

Published By: John James

Copyright © All rights reserved

No part of this publication may be copied, reproduced in any format, by any means electronic or otherwise, without prior consent from the copyright owner and publisher of this book.

Table of Contents

Real Estate Investing

Introduction 10
Chapter 1: Getting into Real Estate Investing 12
Chapter 2: How Market Conditions Can Determine
Your Investment 17
Chapter 3: How to Find Properties to Make You
Money in Real Estate 22
Chapter 4: How to Finance Your Investment 30
Chapter 5: How to Purchase Your First Property in
Real Estate 36
Chapter 6: How Brokers and Property Managers Can
Make Your Job Easier 41
Chapter 7: Protecting Your Assets 46
Chapter 8: How to Handle Your Lease When
Renting out Properties 50
Chapter 9: How to Avoid Common Mistakes 56
Conclusion 62

Stock Market Investing

Introduction 66
Chapter 1: The Right Mindset Makes All the
    Difference 67
Chapter 2: Picking Out Stocks to Invest In 73
Chapter 3: How to Purchase Stocks 81
Chapter 4: What Options Do I Have For Stock
    Market Investing? 85
Chapter 5: Picking Out Your Investment Strategy 92
Chapter 6: Different Styles That Expert Traders Use
    for Stock Trading 103
Chapter 7: Rules That Help to Reduce Your Risks
    When Investing in the Stock Market 109
Conclusion 117

Cryptocurrency

Introduction 121
Chapter 1: What Are Cryptocurrencies? 123

What is A Cryptocurrency? 123
But What are they, Really? 126
Why Does Cryptocurrency Matter? 127
Is There a Future in Cryptocurrency? 132
Why Should I Invest in Cryptocurrency Now? 133

Chapter 2: Choosing A Cryptocurrency 135

Bitcoin 135
Ethereum 136
Ripple 137
Litecoin 138
Monero 139
Making an Investment Choice 140
Making the Choice for Purchasing 141

Chapter 3: Buying and Storing Cryptocurrencies 142

How Does Buying Work? 142
Buying Your First Coins 143
How Does Storing Work? 145
Storing Your New Coins 146
To Summarize 149

Chapter 4: Tips for Mastering Cryptocurrency
Investing and Trading 151

Buy with Funds You Don't Need 151
Research First, Buy and Trade Second 153
Diversify Only If You Understand 154
Pay Attention to the Market Cap 156
You Don't Have to Buy a Whole Coin 156
Unless Circumstances Change, Don't Take Profits 157

Cryptocurrency is Not for Day Traders 158
Buy Low, Sell High, And… 159
Buy Now 160
Buy the Rumor, Sell the News 161
Practice and Get Comfortable 162

Conclusion 163

Real Estate Investing

The Ultimate Beginners' Guide to Real Estate Investing

© Copyright 2018 by John James - All rights reserved.

The following eBook is reproduced below with the goal of providing information that is as accurate and reliable as possible. Regardless, purchasing this eBook can be seen as consent to the fact that both the publisher and the author of this book are in no way experts on the topics discussed within and that any recommendations or suggestions that are made herein are for entertainment purposes only. Professionals should be consulted as needed prior to undertaking any of the action endorsed herein.

This declaration is deemed fair and valid by both the American Bar Association and the Committee of Publishers Association and is legally binding throughout the United States.

Furthermore, the transmission, duplication or reproduction of any of the following work including specific information will be considered an illegal act irrespective of whether it is done electronically or in print. This extends to creating a secondary or tertiary copy of the work or a recorded copy and is only allowed with express written consent from the Publisher. All additional rights reserved.

The information in the following pages is broadly considered to be a truthful and accurate account of facts and, as such, any inattention, use or misuse of the information in question by the reader will render any resulting actions solely under their purview. There are no scenarios in which the publisher or the original author of this work can be in any fashion deemed liable for any

hardship or damages that may befall them after undertaking information described herein.

Additionally, the information in the following pages is intended only for informational purposes and should thus be thought of as universal. As befitting its nature, it is presented without assurance regarding its prolonged validity or interim quality. Trademarks that are mentioned are done without written consent and can in no way be considered an endorsement from the trademark holder.

Introduction

Congratulations on downloading this book and thank you for doing so.

The following chapters will discuss everything that you need to know in order to get started with investing in real estate. This is a great way to make some money and have a lot of fun at the same time. And there are so many options that you can make in this investment that you could easily diversify your whole portfolio and still keep it inside of this market.

This guidebook is going to take some time to look at how to work in real estate. We will talk about how to get started in this industry, how to find the funding that your investment needs, how to work with a property manager and a real estate broker, how to pick out the lease for your investment, and so much more. There are many aspects that come with working in real estate and it often depends on what kind of property you are planning on using and whether you would like to flip that property or rent it out to others. This guidebook will help you out no matter what you plan to do with this investment.

When you are ready to start putting your money to work for you and making a profit in the real estate market, make sure to check out this guidebook and learn everything that you need in order to get started today.

There are plenty of books on this subject on the market,

thanks again for choosing this one! Every effort was made to ensure it is full of as much useful information as possible, please enjoy!

Chapter 1: Getting into Real Estate Investing

While you have a lot of choices to go with when you are ready to start investing your money, real estate can be one of the best options. There are many choices that you can make when you are getting into real estate and there are ways to make money whether the market is doing well or hitting a slump. Each choice is going to provide you with some unique challenges and varying amounts of profit. There is some risk that comes with going into real estate investing and it is going to take some hard work to see results, but there is nothing like working in real estate. Let's take a look at some of the different investment options that you can go with when you are ready to go into real estate.

Residential real estate

The first investment that you can choose is to work with families and individuals who are looking for a place to live. You will offer your property as a rental to them and earn an income from what these families and individuals pay. There are many different types of residential real estate and each one will have a different amount of work and a different amount of profit along the way. Some of the residential properties that you can consider include houses, vacation homes, apartments, and townhomes.

You will find that each one has some benefits. Homes can be popular because there are usually families who will rent them out and most families will stay around for at least a few years, helping you to get a steady stream of income. But some investors like to go with apartments because these can generate more income since they hold more people at once.

Commercial real estate

This is going to include options like office buildings and other similar spaces. When you go into commercial real estate, you will need to find funding to help you construct buildings that will have individual offices for companies and businesses to purchase. While a company is using the building, they will pay you rent. Often these buildings are going to come with leases that are meant to last a few years because most businesses want to get a good deal and do not want to move frequently. This may cost a little more to get started, but it can provide you with a steady stream of income.

Industrial real estate

The next option that you can go with is known as industrial real estate. This one is going to include investments like distribution centers, storage units, and car washes. It can include any kind of real estate that is going to be built for a special purpose and will generate income for the customers who are using the facility. You must remember that these have bigger upfront costs, but the revenue stream is going to be really steady and you will not have to add in a lot of work along the way to keep them going.

Retail real estate

With these investments, you are going to work with options like strip malls, shopping malls, and retail storefronts. There are a lot of businesses willing to pay rent for these spaces, especially if you can place that retail space in an area that has a lot of high traffic. Sometimes the lease is going to include a monthly payment from the tenants, although you can create a lease that will give you a percentage of the sales that your tenants earn while they are in your building. The second option can be nice if you place the building in a good area and your tenants make a lot of money.

These retail spaces are expensive to get started because you need to purchase a lot of land in a busy area and the building is usually pretty big as well. But if you get the right kind of space, you will be able to add in several tenants to that building and earn a bigger income. You can also have some choice in the size of the retail space that you want to go with in order to help determine how much you want to spend and how many tenants you will be able to get into the building.

Mixed use real estate

A good option to go with when you want to make money in real estate is to work with mixed use real estate. This is when you combine a few of the categories above into one project. You must have some good assets to make this work, but they bring out an amazing return on investment if you are able to get people to rent out the building.

An example of doing this is when you invest in building a mixed office building that will hold your main tenants and then you have it surrounded by some retail shops. You would be able to rent it all out. You can even make office buildings with a few stories to rent out more offices or to rent out as apartments. Turn the retail spaces into restaurants, gyms, grocery stores, and so on, and you can really fill up the spaces in no time.

Flipping homes

If you do not feel that holding on to a property and renting it out to other companies or individuals is the right option for your investment needs, it may be a good idea to consider flipping homes. When flipping homes, you do not have to hold on to a building or be a landlord. To make it work, you will need to find a property that is in a good area and for a good price. Usually there is some reason why the property is being offered way under value. Sometimes it is that way because it needs a ton of work, but sometimes you can find one that will only need a bit of work and will be easy to flip.

Flipping a home can turn out to be a tricky investment. While you own that property, you are going to be responsible for making the monthly payments, taking care of insurance, fixing up the home, and any other payments that will come with maintaining the home. This is why it's important to get a good deal on the home and pick out a decent home that you will actually be able to sell later on. Once you purchase the home, you need to make sure that you are able to keep your costs as low as possible and that you can fix it up quickly, so it can get back on the market in no time. The better you are able to stick with these goals the more money you will be able to make. Those who are good at flipping homes will be able to make a lot of money with this investment.

Real estate investing is a great opportunity because it offers so many options for you to choose from. Based on your personal preferences when it comes to investing and how much risk you would like to take, there are different options that can help you get the return on investment you want. Before getting into the market, consider some of these real estate investment types so that you can come up with the winning strategy.

Chapter 2: How Market Conditions Can Determine Your Investment

Many new investors are excited to get started in real estate. They may hear about others who have gotten into this investment and made a lot of money in the process. But before you decide to jump into this investment, it is important that you understand how it works. And the first step is to learn how the market in your area is, so you can make smart decisions.

There are various different markets when it comes to the real estate market. There will be certain times when people are actively searching for homes and you will find that house prices are really high. This is when you will want to consider selling a property or adjusting your rental prices to get the most money possible. Then there are times when the demand for homes is low. This can be a good time to purchase a home because you are more likely to get a good discount on the price. These different phases can happen throughout the year, but often you will want to watch out for the overall trends from one year to another.

There are many times when the market conditions around the real estate industry are going to really influence when you should make purchases, when you are able to sell, and so much more. Each market is going to go through these cycles, no matter how great the area is. There is not always going to be a high demand for homes and you may enter into a cycle where selling homes can be hard. If you happen to purchase a home during these downtimes and they don't reverse quickly, you at least have the option of using your property for rent money to offset some of the costs until the market turns around.

Now, it can be confusing as a beginner to determine when you should get into the market to help you to make the most money and to make sure of the market cycle. Remember that you are able to consider this type of investment no matter what type of market cycle you are in because it is always going to go in a cycle that you can use to your advantage. Some of the different parts of the market cycle that you should learn to recognize to help you make the right decisions on this investment include:

- The peak: The peak is going to be when prices are at an all-time high. At this time, the inventory of available properties is going to be low, which is why the high demand raises the prices so much. In fact, there are often so many interested buyers that a single home, even if it is not in the best shape, will have more than one offer on it. As an investor, this is not the time for you to enter the market because you will pay way more for the home than you will be able to make off it later on. However, if you already own a home and have finished fixing it up, this is an amazing time to sell it.
- The tipping point: This is the point where home prices are too high and the demand for homes is starting to go down. The prices are going to start falling, which will allow the prices to compensate for the high prices and the overbuilding that occurred in the other part of the cycle. There are

times when foreclosure rates are going to go up and some homeowners will have some issues with paying their mortgage because the payments are too high. And then these homeowners will have some issues with selling their home because the value of the home is less than they owe and there are not many interested buyers.

- The decline: This part of the cycle is where the prices of the homes in your area are going to continue to fall. You may notice that you are in this phase when you see many foreclosures going on in the market. People are scared about purchasing homes right now because they do not want to make a purchase that they are not able to afford. With all the foreclosures, there is going to be a lot of inventory on the market that will drive the prices down even further.
- The bottom: This is where the home prices are going to start to even out quite a bit. This part of the cycle will show the lowest prices of the entire thing. If you are looking to get into the market, this is the point where you would want to purchase a property or two because you will get a huge discount. There are many homeowners who are desperate to sell their homes and get at least something out of the deal. You will have a lot of inventory to look through and you will be able to get a good price, which will save you money and help increase your profits later on.
- The climb: The bottom is not going to last forever. There will be a time when buyers will start to gain more confidence in the market and they will start

looking for homes to purchase again. This will help add more sales in real estate in the area and can result in less inventory. Slowly, the price will start to go up.

As you can see, this is a cycle that will keep on going. You need to learn how to read these different parts of the cycle in order to help you to purchase the property at the right time and then sell it at the right time to earn as much money as possible. If you make a purchase of a home during the peak, then you are going to spend so much more money on the property and you will not be able to make any money in the process because it is unlikely the prices will go up higher.

Now, before you get into the market, it is important to figure out where in the market your current area is. If you notice that your area is at the tipping point, this is probably not a good time to make a purchase because prices are high and interested buyers are low. You won't make much of a profit off these properties. But if you notice that your area is at the bottom and there seems to be more confidence in the real estate market, you may want to make a purchase while the prices are low and deals are good. The hope here is that by the time you make some of the adjustments to the house and finish with closing, the market will be into more of a climb or in the peak, and you can profit even more from that.

While you can take some time to learn more about the market cycle and how it works, one of the best ways to recognize the signs of the market is to gain experience.

You may find that it is hard to do this in the beginning, but as you work in the market and start to get involved with the investment, it will become so much easier to learn when you should enter and when you should sell.

While some investors will just go right out there and try to find a property in the beginning, the best investors are the ones who understand that the market is going to really determine if they are going to really get a discount on the home and even when they are able to sell the property when they are done. Learn the different parts of the market cycle and you are sure to get the best profit possible.

Chapter 3: How to Find Properties to Make You Money in Real Estate

There are a lot of things to consider when you are ready to get into the real estate market. You want to make sure that you are able to get the money to purchase a property, that you will be able to maintain that property while you own it, and decide whether you would like to flip that property or use it to make a rental income. When you are ready to get started in this market, you need to be able to pick out the right strategy that will help you make money. For example, you are going to need to do things differently if you want to flip a home compared to what you would do if you wanted to rent out the home. Let's take a look at some of the strategies that you can follow when it is time to purchase your first property in real estate.

Buy and hold strategy

So, the first strategy we are going to look at is known as the buy and hold strategy. This is one of the most common options that you can go with when you are ready to make money in real estate. For this strategy, you are going to find a property that is selling for a good price, and then you will make changes to it before renting it out to others to use. This is an easy form of investing because you may not have to do as much work with it and you can keep making the income year after year. People are going to be willing to pay you good rates for rent as long as you keep the property nice and you take care of them.

There are a lot of advantages that come with using the buy and hold investment strategy. One advantage is that you are able to make some income each month. As long as you were able to get the home for a good discount, you will be able to charge a rent that is high enough to cover the mortgage, the insurance, and anything else that you owe on the house. So, not only are you making a little bit of income in the process, but you are also able to pay down your mortgage and earn equity in the home at the same time. You can choose to use this equity to your advantage later on if you want to purchase more properties or if you would like to hold on to more of the profit if you sell the home later on.

Getting started with the buy and hold strategy is going to require a little bit of legwork. You can't go out and purchase the first home you see or you will end up with a mortgage that is too high for you to cover with rent prices. There are a lot of beginners who will go out and search for a home and who will then make some bad deals because they don't know which homes to look for or what price point they need to stick with. First, make sure you calculate how much you will have to spend on the home to make it livable. This will include the mortgage and the insurance on the home as well as how much money you need to put towards it to fix the property up. Then figure out how much rent you will need to charge to cover all this plus give you some profits. If this amount is not in line with the rent prices in your area, then the property is not a good investment.

You also need to make sure that you are willing to take the

necessary steps to maintain the property. This means you are willing to fix things when they are broken, keep the property looking nice, and pick out tenants that are going to treat your property with respect along the way. There are a lot of decisions that go into picking out a property that works with the buy and hold strategy outside of just grabbing the first house that comes up on the market.

In order to make sure you are able to use this strategy successfully, you will need to learn about the market cycles that we discussed a little bit before. When you start to notice that the properties in your area are getting to a low point (or when the prices of these properties are low because there is a lot of available inventory), then this is the time when you would purchase a property for this strategy. Then, once you start to see that the market is beginning to go back up again, you will avoid making any purchases of these properties because their prices will be too high for you to earn money with this strategy.

Now, some people go into the buy and hold strategy because they want to hold on to them and have some rental properties. They have no plans to sell the properties at all; they just want to have these rental properties in their portfolio. This is a great way to make money, and it is still important for you to consider the market cycle to make it work. If you can purchase a property when the market is at a low point for prices, it will be much easier to find a good deal on a home and it is easier to offer competitive rent while still making a profit.

On the other hand, there are some investors who know that

they need to get a good deal on a property in order to sell it for a good profit. The best time to purchase the property will be during one of those downturns in the market. But sometimes it can take a while before the market goes back up. This does not happen all the time and can result in a few years passing before the market goes up enough to make a profit on that home.

Instead of holding on to that property and paying the mortgage and taxes without any profit, these investors may consider temporarily renting out their homes. They can then make a profit on the rent, but then, when the market goes back up again, they can stop renting and instead sell the home. This is a great way to make sure you can earn as much on the properties while still getting a good deal on them.

Now, you can also choose to use this strategy while holding on to more than one property at a time. This will increase the amount of profit you will make each month because you will be able to combine the income from all the properties together. Most beginners are going to start with just one property, though, to help them learn the ropes and because that's probably all the money they have available. Once you get one property paid down and you have some equity available, you can consider bringing more properties into the mix to help you earn more money.

Flipping properties

Another popular option that you can choose for investing in real estate is known as property flipping. This is the type of real estate investment that you would see on some of those popular home improvement shows, but be aware that a lot of hard work goes into a house flip and you are not likely to make hundreds of thousands of dollars on each flip like they do on television. But, as an investor, if you are good at finding some deals on a home and you are ready to get your hands dirty, then this is a great way to make money in real estate.

The idea behind flipping properties is that you need to find a good property that has many features that a seller is looking for but there is something wrong with it that causes its worth and price to be lower than it should be. Sometimes the things that make the price of the property low are really simple fixes and you can quickly turn things around and make a large profit. Sometimes it may just be as simple as someone needing to get rid of the property quickly. You would find this good deal, purchase the property, do a few improvements, and then sell it to make a profit. Hopefully things would work out so that you would be able to sell the property for a comparable price to other homes in the area, so it would be easier for you to sell it as well.

Most investors who go into flipping homes will focus on a single family home since these are the easiest to use with this option. A good rule of thumb that you can use for flipping homes is the 70% rule. With this one, you will only purchase homes that are being sold for 70% of their current value, less any of the costs of rehab. For example, let's say that a home is worth $100,000 in its current area if it were sold in good condition, but you are going to have to put about $20,000 into it to make it look nice. According to the rule of 70%, you would not purchase this home for more than $50,000 to make a good profit. You could then make the adjustments to the home and then sell it for that $100,000 when you are done. Remember this is just something to consider and picking out the home that you will use, while also considering the costs, will vary depending on each unique situation.

When you are flipping homes and you want to make some good money, you need to learn how to be fast. The longer you have the property after you make the purchase the more money you end up spending on that property in the form of insurance, taxes and a mortgage. And then you need to add to this the costs of fixing up the home. When figuring out how much money you need to flip the home, remember that you need to calculate all the things above for at least a few months. It will take some time to make the fixes you want, and most homes will sit on the market for a few months before they sell.

When doing your calculations, you can consider using the property as a rental. This is a good idea if you are worried about the market staying at the low point for some time but you don't want to miss out on a good deal on a property. But as soon as you purchase the property, start advertising that it is for rent, even while you are fixing it up. It takes some time to find interested renters and you need to screen them all before you let them onto the property.

There is a lot of work that comes with the job of flipping homes and you must be an active participant in it all. You need to find a good deal on a property, find the right funding, and fix up the property as quickly as possible so you can get it listed on the market again as soon as possible.

Wholesaling

This is an option that can make you some good money in real estate, but it is not one that a lot of investors know about. With this particular strategy, you are going to work to find some good deals on a property, write out a contract that lets you have that deal, and then you will be able to sell that contract to another investor or someone else who is interested in that property. In most cases, the wholesaler is never technically going to own the property, just the contract. Instead, they are in charge of looking around for some good properties and then will get them set up for another person to make the purchase. The investor or other person who ends up purchasing the contract will pay the amount of the contract along with a fee for the work the wholesaler does.

There are many ways in which the wholesaler will be able to sell off these contracts. Sometimes they will be able to sell their contracts to some retail buyers, but often these contracts will go to some investors, such as other house flippers, who are known to be cash buyers. When dealing with a cash buyer, the wholesaler will get the benefit of not having to wait for the bank to close on a deal, saving a lot of time and hassle.

Many investors like working as a wholesaler because it is

known to be one of the easiest investment options in the real estate market. You will not need to worry about as many upfront costs and the wholesaler doesn't technically own the property at any time, so they won't have to worry about the costs of fixing up the property, loan fees, contractors, tenants, and banks. The potential profit is not as high as house flipping or a good rental property, but there is less risk and if you are good at finding discount properties, it can help you to make some good money.

While there are a lot of good benefits to working with wholesaling, there is some work and a few risks with choosing this option. The wholesaler must always be on the lookout for a good deal so that they have inventory ready to sell to their contacts. They need to also have a good funnel for marketing so that they can attract the right leads during this time. And once you have a property contract, you must be able to find buyers who actually want the property as well or you will end up owning the property yourself.

Wholesaling is often touted as a method of investing in real estate that doesn't need any money. While you are able to work on the contracts and sell them without having to use any money, you do need to have some financial resources in order to create the marketing funnel to reach both the sellers and the buyers. But if you are successful at finding the right marketing tunnel for your needs and you can provide some good deals to investors, you can make a great income from this option without spending a lot of money on startup costs.

Chapter 4: How to Finance Your Investment

If you have ever taken a look at the home prices in your area, you know that it is going to take some serious capital to get started with investing in real estate. Most homes are going to cost over $100,000, even at a discount. And then you will need to fix up many of them before you are able to sell them or rent them out. Now, you will not necessarily need to have all that money on hand to get started. You can take out a mortgage from the bank, but this can take some time to work with and you will be responsible for bank fees and for interest until you are able to sell the property.

Since most people do not have enough money on them or saved up to finance the purchase of a property, there are a few financing options that the investor is able to choose from to get started. These are going to make it easier to get some of the money that you need to purchase the property as well as providing you with funds to make some improvements to the property as well. However, you must make sure that you are prepared before you ask for funding.

Banks, portfolio lenders, and some other options are willing to provide you with some funds, but they want to make sure that they will be able to get their investment back. You need to have your finances in order, a good business plan in place, a good credit score, and even a marketing plan before you even go to talk to some of these groups.

The good news is the first property is going to be the hardest to fund. You will have to prove that you will be a good person for this investment without any proof. After you have done this a few times, the banks and lenders will be able to tell that you know what you are doing, and you will have some cash behind you to use as well, so it becomes easier to keep on going.

But if you are a beginner who doesn't have a ton of capital to work with, it is important to search for a good lender who is willing to give you a chance and will give you the funds you need at a good rate. Some of the different funding options you can go with include:

Conventional mortgage

The first option that you may want to go with is known as a conventional mortgage. This is a good one to go with because it allows you to get started with a certain percentage down. The regular conventional loan will ask for twenty percent down on the property, but there are some other options you can pursue that will allow you to start with a lower down payment. The conventional mortgage can take more work, but they often provide the lowest interest rates and the best terms to work with.

When you are looking into a conventional mortgage, you are going to be responsible for doing much of the legwork. You must provide them with a lot of information about yourself to help them determine if you will be able to pay the mortgage back. You should prove your income history, your assets, that you have a good credit score, and that you are able to handle all your current debts while holding on to the new mortgage. Depending on the bank you go to, there may be some additional information that they will require from you, but start by filling out an application and go from there with the bank.

To help increase your chances of getting the funding you need, it is best to go with a bank that you already do business with, or at least one that is local to your area. This helps because they often want to help out new businesses in their area and they may already have some of the required information about you that they need.

203K loans

This is another option you can go with and it is part of the popular FHA loans. It will allow you as the investor to purchase a new property that needs some work. It not only allows you to get funds to purchase the home, but it provides you with some funds to help repair the home as well. All of these will be wrapped up into one loan, rather than having to take out several at the same time, so you will only have one payment to worry about.

Hard money

You can also choose to go with a financing option that is known as hard money. With this option, you will get financing from private businesses and individuals who know that you plan to invest in real estate with that money. There are some different terms that you can use with this kind of funding, but you and the other party will be able to come up with the specifics between yourselves. Some of the common terms and conditions that come with this kind of funding include:

- The loan you receive must be based on the value of the property and how much it is worth.
- These loans are usually not long-term loans. You will be expected to pay them back within 6 months to 3 years.
- The rate of interest you will pay on these loans will be much higher than traditional loans.
- There is going to be a high loan point on these loans. What this means is you will need to pay a lot of fees on these loans.
- Most lenders who are giving out this money will need you to verify what income you make.
- You will find that most lenders for this are not going to take the time to pull up your credit score and this transaction is not going to show up on your credit report.
- These loans can be funded quickly, which can be nice if you want to jump on a deal quickly.
- Most of the time the lenders have the understanding that you will need to do a bit of work on the property before they can earn their money back.

If you want to flip a home and you would like to make sure that you can get the money quickly, you will find that working with a hard money loan is a great option for you. But you need to get the work on the home done quickly and sell the home fast because the terms of these loans are not going to last long.

Private money

You can also choose to work with private money. This kind of funding is slightly different than working with hard money lending. This is because hard lenders are professional investors and they expect you to follow the terms directly for the investment. With a private money lender, there is more flexibility. These lenders are just getting into the market and want you to do the work in real estate while they make the profit. In some cases, you and the private lender can have a close relationship as well.

Partnerships

Depending on your credit score and your finances, it may be hard for you to find the funding you need to get into real estate all on your own. You may not make enough income, have too much debt or not enough money to put in as a down payment and so the bank refuses your application. If this is the case for you, it may be worth your time to consider getting into a partnership with someone else who wants to enter real estate investing to increase your chances of getting funding.

You will find that the bank will look more favorably on your request for funding when you are in a partnership. This is because they now have the ability to hold two people responsible for paying that money back, and they are more likely to get at least some of the money back. The bank will be able to count the income from both individuals and this makes the debt to income ratio easier to manage. Of course, when you work in a partnership, you will need to share the profits, but it can certainly help when you have to share in the work.

Before you decide to go with a partnership, you must make sure that you are picking the right person to go into this partnership with. You need someone with a good credit history, someone who has a good income, and someone who is actually going to be there to help you with the work. Picking someone who is missing some of these things can make it hard to get the funding you need and may leave you doing most of the work on the property while still sharing the profits.

While the ideal situation is to use all of your own money to make the purchases because this can be the easiest, it costs the least amount because you won't have to pay interest or other fees, and you can keep all of the profit. But purchasing a home can be expensive and many real estate investors don't have that kind of money set aside to get started. Using one of these other forms of investing can make it easier to get the money you need so you can purchase your home, rent it out or flip it, and start making money in real estate.

Chapter 5: How to Purchase Your First Property in Real Estate

At this point, you have probably taken some time to look at the market in your area and even talked to a few sources for funding and gotten that in place as well. Now that this is all organized, it is time to start taking the necessary steps in order to purchase your first property. There are some specific steps that you should take to ensure that you get a property at a good price, with little work required on it, so that you can get everything done and still make a good profit in the process. When you have decided that it is time to purchase that very first investment property, make sure that you are going through the following steps:

- First, you must pick out the strategy you would like to use. This is going to make it easier to determine which properties you would like to purchase. Rental properties versus flipping properties will have different requirements.
- You should also define what your selection criteria are. What exactly do you want to find in your property? Would you like this property to be in a certain location? What is the price you want to stick with? Do you want to rent out to a family or an individual? How much work are you able to put into the property after you make the purchase? Having this information figured out ahead of time will help you to pick the right property without having to worry about getting distracted during

your search.

- Pick out the financing you want to use. Since most people are not going to have the full amount of a property saved up when they purchase in real estate, you will often need to rely on a bank or another source for your funding. You can take the time while you are searching, but before you put in an offer, to get pre-approved for your loan.
- Look through online sites, the MLS, yard signs, classifieds, and even direct mail in order to see which properties are currently for sale in your area. You can do this on your own, although some individuals choose to work with a realtor to help them find the property they want. With each property you see, you must run it through the criteria you set in the earlier steps to make sure it is the right property for your needs. It is always a good idea to allow for a bit of wiggle room in case there is a property that is really good but slightly out of your criteria, but stick as close to them as possible.
- Make an offer. You can work with a realtor on this one. This is a good idea as a beginner purchasing your first home. The seller is going to be the one who pays the realtor, so it will not cost you anything at this point. Realtors are trained to handle all the legal stuff of the house selling process, so they can be a good resource. There are some strategies you can use when purchasing a home and it depends on how much the seller wants for the property and how much you are able to pay. You should start out with a little bit of wiggle room

here because the seller is likely going to want to negotiate on the price. Starting out at your maximum pretty much means that you are going to lose out.

- Negotiate. The seller is going to want to do some back and forth with you to get the best price they can. You should start out at an offer that is below what you are willing to spend so that the seller can negotiate with you. If the seller takes the first offer, you got a really good offer. If they counter, then you have some room to come back. When the seller takes your offer, the realtor will be able to help you write out the purchase agreement. If you are doing this on your own, you can print out a purchase agreement on your own as well.
- While you are waiting for the funding to come through, and after the seller has agreed to your offer, you must make sure that you go through and do all the proper inspections. This can give you a good idea of what issues are already present and need to be fixed on the property. Depending on the issue and the agreement between you and the seller, you may even be able to get the seller to handle some of the repairs, which will save you time and money. If you skip these inspections, you are the one who will be on the hook for getting them all fixed on your own. Assume that the person you will sell the house to will do inspections, so, by doing one now, you can avoid some issues in the future inspection.
- During this time, you should also start talking to contractors who can help you get the work done.

As soon as the loan and funding come through, the clock will start ticking. The longer you hold on to the property the more it is going to cost you as you make mortgage payments and more. You want to try to get quotes for how much it will cost to do the work and then see if you can get the contractors into the home as soon as possible after the closing. If you plan it all out, it may be possible to get the work done on the property within a few weeks, so you can relist it, or start renting it out, very quickly.

- Once you have completed all the inspections and you are happy with how they were handled, it is time to go to the Title and Escrow office to sign all the papers that are needed. Then the paperwork is going to be recorded and you are technically the owner of the home. You can start to get the home ready, get the contractors in, and start planning for how you will make a profit on the home. If you are going to rent it out, you can start listing the property for new tenants. If you plan to sell it, get the work done quickly so that you can list it and get it sold. All of this needs to be done as quickly as possible.

One thing to remember is that you are usually given a little bit of a reprieve before your first payment is due. You can usually make it about two months before you need to send in the first payment. Depending on your agreement with the bank, you may be able to pay a little extra in interest at closing and get the payment period extended a little bit longer. Use this to your advantage to get the work done quickly without having to make payments on the home and hopefully save money in the process.

The process is going to work pretty similar to this when talking about residential or commercial real estate as well. You must always make sure that you are getting a good deal on the property that you pick, and it is important to do inspections to make sure that nothing is hidden in the property that could make you lose money. But if you follow your criteria and work with the right people who can take care of all the legal stuff, you will soon own a real estate investment and can decide what you would like to do with it to turn it into a money maker.

Chapter 6: How Brokers and Property Managers Can Make Your Job Easier

As someone who has just gotten started in real estate, you may want to consider working with some experts in the field to help you get going. There are many people you will need to work with in order to help you to purchase the property, rent the property, sell the property, fix up the property, and so much more. While it may make things easier if you were able to do it all on your own, this is just not something you will be able to do when you get into real estate. Working with property managers and real estate brokers can make your life so much easier and can help you to earn a lot of profit in this industry. Let's learn more about both groups of people to see how they will be able to help your real estate investment.

The real estate broker

The first person you will want to consider working with is a real estate broker. When it is time to buy or sell a property, it is often a good idea to work with a real estate broker. There are a lot of benefits to working with one of these brokers and, while you do need to pay them for their work, it actually will make it easier to come out ahead on your investment.

First, you can use a broker when you are ready to purchase a new property. Your real estate broker is often the first person an investor will call in order to help them find the property they want to use. These brokers know the area that you want to purchase in and are able to give some great insights about the prices in that area and where they will go in the near future. They also have all the connections that you need around town to find those great deals. These brokers seem to know everyone in the town and can get you to those deals long before anyone else can. You can try to do this all on your own, but you will find that it is much easier to work with a real estate broker.

Once you have found the property you would like to purchase, your broker will still be able to help you out. They are good at handling all the legal paperwork that is needed when it is time to put in an offer and do some negotiations along the way until a price is agreed upon. The broker will help you to walk through all this paperwork and can even point you to some suggestions about doing the inspections, and who to hire as a contractor, and can basically ensure that you are able to get into the new property as soon as possible.

After you purchase the new property and fix it up, or even after you have rented it out for some time and are finally ready to sell it after a few years, it is time to get the property ready to sell. You will be amazed at the difference a real estate broker can make when it comes to selling the home. There are some investors who try to save money and sell the house on their own, but real estate brokers are more efficient at getting property sold and are well worth the money.

When you are ready to go find a broker to work with on this adventure, you need to find one who is not only qualified to do the job but also one you can get along with. Real estate investing is something you can stick with for a long time and working with the same real estate broker can make the process easier. It can be nice to work with the same person throughout it all rather than having to restart the process with a new agent each time you want to purchase or sell a property.

Working with a property manager on your rentals

Rental properties are a great way to make money over the long term, especially if you are able to get a good deal on a property and you can pay down some of the mortgage. As you accumulate more rental properties, you are able to make more money in the process. Over time, you may decide that it is too much work for you to do all the stuff for each rental property such as collecting the rent, cleaning the homes, looking for new tenants and more. This is when you may want to consider hiring a property manager.

These property managers can help you to take care of all your rental properties so that you can concentrate on doing other things. They know how to run these rental properties and will make sure that you get your money out of each one. Yes, it does mean you will have to share some of your profits with them, but it also means you will not have to put in as much work on the properties.

When you are ready to pick out a good property manager to work with, some of the things to look for include:

- The first thing you should look at is how many

properties that manager is in charge of. You want to make sure that they are not taking on too many other properties or they may run into trouble having time to manage yours as well. If a property manager seems to have a large number of properties they are in charge of, it is best to go with someone else.

- How much the manager charges. You also want to make sure that you are getting a good deal with a property manager who will not overcharge you. Most property managers will ask for seven to ten percent of your rental revenue on the properties they will look over. If you are talking to a manager who is asking for a number that is way off from this, then it is best to avoid them.

- What software the manager decides to use. A property manager is able to use different software programs to keep track of their costs and to collect the rent. You can check out the software and see if it will actually be able to do its job.

- Ask if the manager does inspections. You want to pick out a property manager who is willing to do routine inspections of your properties. You also want to make sure that they are not charging a lot of extra fees in order to do these inspections. And when the manager does the inspections, make sure they know the rules and know that they still need to be respectful of your current tenant, such as giving a good amount of notice so the tenant can be prepared. If you find that a manager is making it difficult for you to do a routine inspection to make sure that your properties are doing well, then it is a

good idea to find a new manager.
- You should also make sure that you pick out a property manager you can get along with. There are some property managers who assume they know best and will try to take over control from you. If they won't listen to the way you want to do things, no matter what their experience is, or one of them talks over you, is hard to get ahold of or there is another issue, then there are plenty of other managers you can go with.

While it will eat into your profits a little bit, hiring a good property manager can make all the difference when it comes to taking care of your rental properties. As you grow your portfolio and you get more properties, it can be nice to have someone else who can take care of things so you can concentrate on growing your investment even more.

Chapter 7: Protecting Your Assets

When you decide to invest in real estate, you must understand that you are working on a new business. You may be ready to get the funding and start looking for the properties you want to use to start the investment, but you may not have thought about your investment as the business that it is. If you don't treat this new investment like one of your assets, you are running the potential for some trouble. Say that someone gets harmed on the property, whether it is a contractor or one of your tenants, you will be the one held liable for the injuries and damages. Depending on what kind of business you consider yourself to have you may have to worry about how much the other person could claim against you. Let's take a look at the most common types of businesses and how each one will handle your business.

Sole proprietor

If you go into this investment and you do not pick out an entity for your business, you will automatically be considered a sole proprietor. This is basically an individual who runs their business and who is going to be responsible for all parts of the business. You will probably call the business something with your own name and there isn't going to be a separation of your assets and your liabilities. Some people prefer this because it can help them to keep things simple and there won't be a lot of paperwork that you need to concentrate on. However, if there is some reason for someone to come after your business, then they can also come after some of your personal assets as well.

Limited liability company

This is another option you can choose to go with and it is considered a hybrid between a partnership and a corporation. Members who choose this entity for their business are going to have the flexibility and income benefits that come from being in a partnership or a sole proprietorship, without all the paperwork to deal with like working with a corporation. They will also get the benefit of limiting how much they are liable for if something goes wrong. There are a few legal differences between this and some of the others, so you will need to learn more about these, but this is a good option if you would like to protect some of your personal assets while still getting a lot of freedom in running your business.

Corporation

When you are working with a real estate investment, it is not likely that you will choose to work as a corporation, at least in the beginning. This is because a corporation is a large legal entity that will have to spend a lot of time on paperwork and all the formal stuff in order to get started. You will start with filing articles of incorporation inside your state and then you may have to consider working with stockholders. This can take away some of the freedom of making decisions. There are some benefits to using this kind of entity in your business, such as getting tax deductions to save you money. You do need to be a little bit careful about double taxation. This can occur when you get taxed on your profits and on the stockholder dividends.

S-corporation

This is a good option to go with if you would like to end up with some of the benefits that a corporation gets but you would like to be a small business rather than a large corporation. These are ones that are looking to get some of the tax advantages, as long as they are able to meet the requirements of the IRS. They can wave the corporate taxes and the owners of the company are able to report the income on their personal returns, helping them to avoid issues with being taxed more than once.

Which one should I pick?

For the most part, you will not want to work with a corporation because this is for bigger entities and the double taxation is going to cost you a lot of money, but while the sole proprietor option may seem tempting, you won't want to go with this either because it limits the amount of protection that you are going to get.

For real estate investing, most investors choose to go with the LLC option. This gives them the right mix between the sole proprietorship and the corporation. You will be able to be in control of this form of business entity and you won't have to listen to the views of stockholders to get things done, but you still get the protection of your personal assets with this structure. If you do decide to become a corporation, most of the time it is best to register as an s-corporation because it will save you money from the double taxation that occurs with normal corporations.

As you can see, there are a lot of things to consider when it comes to picking out the entity that you would like to give to your business. Each one has its own benefits and negatives and it often depends on what you would like to do with your business and how much protection you would like to have if something goes wrong.

As a beginner, you may assume that it doesn't matter whether or not you set yourself up as a business entity at all, but there are a lot of things that could happen with one of your properties. What if you hire a contractor who falls or gets hurt on the property or something happens with one of your tenants while they are living in the building? Without the right business entity in place, the individual in question could come after not only your business assets but also your personal assets. But with the help of a good business entity in place, you can protect yourself and deal more with the tasks of running your investment.

Chapter 8: How to Handle Your Lease When Renting out Properties

So far, we have spent some time talking about what you need to do if you are interested in purchasing a home and flipping it for a profit. But what happens if you would like to get a property and use it as a rental? Picking out the lease that you will use with your tenants is an integral part of helping you to keep your properties in good shape, keeping yourself protected, and ensuring that you pick out good tenants. These leases are meant to help protect both you and the tenant and they ensure that both parties know what is expected of them from the beginning. Some of the different types of leases that you can consider for your properties include:

Residential property leases

The first type of lease we are going to take a look at is a residential property lease and this is going to be different from what you would offer to a tenant of a commercial property. Sometimes these leases will change depending on what property you are working with. For example, when you work with a single-family home, you can consider having the tenant pay their own utilities in addition to the rent, while some landlords will lump the utilities into the rent for those living in apartments to make it easier. You can also consider whether you want to write out a short-term or a long-term lease.

The short-tern leases are going to be the ones that are for one year at a time. You can also offer ones that go for a shorter amount of time, like six months. There are even some apartments that are temporary living spaces for those who just need a place for a few months. You will have to spend more time getting tenants to fill the space, but you can also charge a lot more per month for these places than you could if someone stayed for a year or more.

You can also choose to write out leases that are long term. Most people will stick with leases that last one year at a time. Even if they end up staying for longer, they like that flexibility to move out if they would like. But there are others who are willing to stay in the property for two years or more in exchange for receiving a discount on their rent. This provides you with a guarantee of a steady income for two or three years and the tenant will be able to get a discount on what they are paying.

When you are picking out which lease is going to meet your needs the best, you need to consider all of the things you are going to cover. It is common for those who go into a single-family home to find that they need to pay for their own utilities and water and then the landlord would be responsible for things like maintaining the home and paying any taxes. If you are renting out larger complexes, you may find that it is easier to group the utilities together and then add that price to the rental price and the tenants will appreciate having it all combined as well. You should decide which extras, including ones that are not listed above, you are willing to provide to the tenant ahead of time.

Also, the lease needs to list out all of the responsibilities of the tenant. The tenant should be responsible for submitting their rent on time or the landlord will get the right to begin the eviction process. The tenant is also responsible for taking care of the property while they are living inside it and not allowing more than normal wear and tear inside the property. If the tenant does not uphold their rights in the rental agreement, the landlord will have some legal recourse that they can use.

The landlord is also going to have some responsibilities that they need to come up with. For example, if something goes wrong with the property, such as the water not working, the electricity or heat stopping or something similar, then the landlord is responsible for taking care of these right away. Just as the landlord has some legal recourse if the tenant doesn't pay or follow the lease properly, the tenant will have some legal recourse if the landlord does not keep the home properly taken care of.

Commercial property leases

In addition to working with single-family homes and apartments, you can work with commercial properties. These are going to work with slightly different rules that come with the commercial property leases, but this is because you are working with different types of tenants in the process. The terms will depend on what kind of property you are working with, how much the tenants make, and more. Let's take a look at some of the options that you can pick from when it comes to commercial property leases.

Full service lease

The first option you can go with is a full-service lease, which is one that is going to include everything in the rent. The landlord will pay everything on the property for the tenant including the maintenance, insurance, taxes, utilities, janitorial services and more. Before setting the rent, the landlord needs to go through and figure out how much all of that stuff would cost and then they can split it up between how many tenants they will have inside of the building. The landlord can even add in something to the lease that will protect them if one of the tenants uses up too much in utilities.

The rent for one of these will usually be higher because so much is included in the price. But some tenants like this because they can just pay one thing to take care of all their business needs. It keeps things easier, so they are willing to pay a bit more on their rent.

Net lease

Another option you are able to choose when working with commercial property leases is known as a net lease. With a net lease, you are going to charge the tenant a lower lease, and it will include the rental space for the business to use as well as usual costs like maintenance. The tenant will pay this inside of the lease and then the landlord will take care of these costs for the tenant. There are a few options that can fit into this type of lease as well:

- Single net lease: With the single net lease, the tenant will get the benefit of paying the lower base rent, but then they will need to do a pro-rated share of the property tax. This tax is something that all of the tenants will share in based on how much room they are going to take up inside of the building. The landlord will be able to pay for some of the expenses of using the building, but the individual tenants are responsible for some things like utilities and janitorial staff.
- Double net lease: This type of lease is where the tenant is going to be responsible for the base rent that the landlord charges, and then they will need to pay for their part of the property taxes and the insurance. The landlord will still be in charge of paying for all the maintenance requirements of the building, but the tenant will need to pay for the utilities that they use.
- Triple net lease: As a landlord, you may be interested in going with the triple net lease on your commercial properties. With this type of lease, your tenant is going to be in charge of the base rent that you charge each month as well as their property taxes, utilities, common area utilities, janitorial services, insurance, and anything extra they would like to have in their building. This one is going to favor the landlord more than anything because the tenant is basically going to pay for everything, but the tenant may like this because it allows them to be more transparent to their customers.

There are many options that come with picking out a lease with commercial properties and working out the best option that will attract the right companies into the area while still making a good profit. Carefully consider each of these options before deciding to ensure you get the best option for both you and your tenant.

Chapter 9: How to Avoid Common Mistakes

As a beginner, you are trying to get used to the whole idea of working in real estate. You want to be able to earn money back on your investment as soon as possible and you do not want to end up failing in the process. Learn some of the common mistakes that beginners make and how to avoid them. Follow some of the tips below, and you are sure to make a good return on investment in the real estate market in no time.

Forgetting the marketing plan

Real estate investing is just like a business and you need to treat it as such if you want to see success. A marketing plan can help to bring the different parts of the business together and it can really help you to define your goals and your timeline for achieving some of these goals. First, when you approach the bank to get some of the funding that you need, you will be required not only to have information on your income and credit history, but they will also want to see your marketing or business plan to determine whether you are ready.

While a marketing plan may seem like it takes up a lot of time and isn't really necessarily, if you want to see success, you need to have this business plan in place. Consistently, beginners and professionals who have this marketing plan (and who have it all written out) are more likely to find success compared to those who never make one of these plans.

Starting a business or marketing plan can be tough and you may not know where to start. There are several business plans available online that you can use for your needs. Just go online and find the one you like the best and then fill in the blanks to make it relevant for your real estate business.

Not using your available resources

There are actually a lot of different resources available for those who are trying to get into the real estate market. You can work with a real estate agent who will be able to answer your questions and help you to find the right properties or help you sell your property. There are contractors who can help you to get the work done in no time. There are bankers who can point out the best options for loans and resources to make your investments better than before.

As a beginner, there is nothing wrong with using all the resources provided to you. Some of the best investors in the market are using these resources so it makes sense that you should be using them as well. Find the ones that will help out with your particular investing method and stick with them.

The bidding war

It is important that you never go into an investment and get into a bidding war with other interested buyers over the same property. It may be one of the best properties out there, but as soon as you get into a bidding war with others, the discount price that you were going for on that property will go out the window. You can easily get into the mindset that you must have this property and that you can't let someone else have it. And that will play on your emotions, rather than on your logic, and can make it hard to make money in the long term.

If you get into a bidding war and find that others are going for the same property, it is probably best to just let the property go. Otherwise, if the emotions start going and you get stuck in a loop of not wanting to let it go, you are going to end up paying a lot more for the property than you can afford or even more than the property is worth. Remember that bidding wars are great for the seller because they increase the amount they will be able to earn on the home, but they can be a pain for investors who want to get the house for a low price.

Purchasing a home and not seeing it before

It is never a good idea to purchase a home that you have not been able to personally look over yourself. It doesn't matter how good of a deal that property is. It does not matter how the market is doing. It does not matter how much you trust the person who tells you about the property. This is your investment and you need to be active in determining whether this is the right investment for you by seeing that property before purchasing.

Pictures and virtual tours never work out well if you don't

see the property. They are great for the buyer to get a good idea of the layout of the building and to make some decisions about whether this property is even something they are interested in, but the house is going to look much different than the pictures the seller presents. Of course, the seller is going to post pictures that show the home in the best light possible. But when you get to the home, you may notice that the rooms appear smaller, the garage is in a weird location on the property, the neighbor has some loud dogs that bark all day long or other issues that will affect how well you will be able to sell the property or rent it out later on. Always go and see the property in person before you get too attached or decide to purchase the home.

Not understanding your budget

You have to set a budget right from the beginning and learn how to stick with it as closely as possible. And you need to remember all of the things that you need to include in the budget. It is easy to think that it is only going to take you a month or two to get the home ready to sell, but what happens if it takes you six months or longer to sell the home? And did you really calculate all of the costs, not just the mortgage but also the taxes and insurance on the property? And how much is it going to cost to repair the home before you can sell it, and did you leave some cushion room in case things are not going the way you would like them to?

As you can see, things can start to get out of control if you are not careful with your budget. If you purchase the home for more than your budget, you may not be able to recover it later on. If your contractors are not able to stick with your budget or your timeline, it could ruin your budget as well. If it takes longer to sell the home, you may pay more than you had planned.

Come up with a budget and stick to it or leave a little bit of breathing room in case things do not go the way you want. If you are someone who struggles with budgeting in your regular life, it may not be a good idea to get into budgeting when you are dealing with real estate.

Getting into kitchen and bathroom remodels

It is really tempting to get into a new property and think you need to remodel the kitchen and the bathroom. This can be an issue because maybe one or both of these rooms look horrible inside the home and you know that you will never be able to sell the property if you do not make some changes. The biggest issue here is that these kinds of remodels are really expensive and do not give you the return on investment you wish. If you spend $20,000 on remodeling one of these rooms, it may make the house look better, but you would be lucky if it raised the price of the home more than a few thousand dollars.

There are a few things that you can do here. If the kitchen and bathroom need just a few little things to make them look better, such as a quick paint job or taking carpet out of them and adding some tile, then it is worth your time to go for the house (as long as the rest of the repairs are not too extensive) and pay a bit for them. This will help you to sell the house, and if the repairs are small, then you can easily make the money back.

However, if you are looking at these rooms and you feel that you need to replace a lot of things inside of the home, from the flooring to the sinks and counters and everything else, then it is probably best to go with a different house. Many times, you will not be able to sell the home without fixing them, and it is best to let someone else take on the headache.

Working in real estate is something that can take a lot of time and effort in order to see some success. It can provide you with a good profit when you are done, but many new investors do not realize how much time, money, and work they will need to put in to see these profits. Make sure you take a look at some of these common mistakes and figure out how you can avoid them to make the most profit.

Conclusion

Thank you for making it through to the end of this book, let's hope it was informative and able to provide you with all of the tools you need to achieve your goals, whatever they may be.

The next step is to decide what kind of real estate investing you would like to do. There are so many options available to you and to others who would like to get started, but it does take some time and some work. This guidebook took a look at all the different aspects of investing in real estate and what you need to do to get started. From picking out a good property to finding the funding you need to see success, working with a real estate agent, protecting your assets, and setting up leases if you decide to go with rental properties, you are sure to learn everything you need to know in order to get started in real estate investing today!

Finally, if you found this book useful in anyway, a review on Amazon is always appreciated!

Stock Market Investing

The Complete Beginner's Guide to Gain Passive Income by Stock Market Investing (Learn Secret Hints and Tips to Make Your Money Work for You!)

© Copyright 2018 by John James - All rights reserved.

The following eBook is reproduced below with the goal of providing information that is as accurate and reliable as possible. Regardless, purchasing this eBook can be seen as consent to the fact that both the publisher and the author of this book are in no way experts on the topics discussed within and that any recommendations or suggestions that are made herein are for entertainment purposes only. Professionals should be consulted as needed prior to undertaking any of the action endorsed herein.

This declaration is deemed fair and valid by both the American Bar Association and the Committee of Publishers Association and is legally binding throughout the United States.

Furthermore, the transmission, duplication or reproduction of any of the following work including specific information will be considered an illegal act irrespective of if it is done electronically or in print. This extends to creating a secondary or tertiary copy of the work or a recorded copy and is only allowed with express written consent from the Publisher. All additional rights reserved.

The information in the following pages is broadly considered to be a truthful and accurate account of facts and as such any inattention, use or misuse of the information in question by the reader will render any resulting actions solely under their purview. There are no scenarios in which the publisher or the original author of this work can be in any fashion deemed liable for any

hardship or damages that may befall them after undertaking information described herein.

Additionally, the information in the following pages is intended only for informational purposes and should thus be thought of as universal. As befitting its nature, it is presented without assurance regarding its prolonged validity or interim quality. Trademarks that are mentioned are done without written consent and can in no way be considered an endorsement from the trademark holder.

Introduction

Congratulations on downloading this book and thank you for doing so.

The following chapters will discuss everything you need to know to get started with investing in the stock market. While some people will choose to start their own businesses, work on their retirements, or work in real estate investing, there is nothing that works as well, and provides the return on investment, as when you work in the stock market.

This guidebook will talk about everything that you need to know to get started with investing in the stock market. We will talk about the mindset that you need to see success with the stock market investment, how to pick out stocks that will provide a good return on investment, how to enter the stock market, how to pick good strategies, and how to reduce your risk. Whether you have been an investor in the past or not, this guidebook will help you to get started in the stock market.

There are plenty of books on this subject on the market, thanks again for choosing this one! Every effort was made to ensure it is full of as much useful information as possible, please enjoy!

Chapter 1: The Right Mindset Makes All the Difference

When it comes to investing your money and putting it to work for you, there are several opportunities that you can choose from. Each person has their own personal style when it comes to these investments and picking out the one that is best for their needs. Some people might like to get their hands dirty and follow the market with real estate investing. Some like to play it safe and will just put their money into a retirement plan. And others will choose to work with the stock market.

Often it will depend on how much time you have to devote to the investment, how much money you can put towards the investment, and how much risk you are willing to take. Of course, the more risk you are willing to take, the more money you could potentially make. There is also the risk of losing more money, which is why you need to find the perfect balance between how much you can earn with an investment and how much you could lose with that investment if things go wrong.

While there are a lot of different investment opportunities that you can choose from, such as real estate investing, investing in bonds, starting your own business and more, you can also work with the stock market. This type of investment will include you taking your money and investing it to help another company grow. In return for investing in a company that does well, you will earn dividends each quarter, or part of the profit that the company brings in. Or you could get into the process of buying the stocks at a lower price and selling them when the price goes up so that you can make a profit.

Those are the two most common ways to make money in the stock market, but there are many others that you can work with as well. With all the options available for investing in the stock market, it is no wonder that a lot of people choose to go with this option. You will be able to take a look at how much time, money, and risk you have available and choose which stocks, as well as which strategies, will be the best for you. Depending on which stocks you go with, it is even possible to start making a profit without all the wait.

It is exciting to get into the stock market and see how things can go for you, but some people want to weigh all their options and make sure that they can actually make money rather than losing out on money. When you are ready to start entering the stock market, and you want to make a good income from your investment, make sure to learn the right strategies that will ensure that you see success.

Starting off in the stock market

Before you decide to jump right into stock market investing, you must take some time to determine what your goals are for doing this kind of investing. If you jump into this investment without thinking it through, you will fail miserably. You should know where you want to start out at as well as why you are doing the investment. Do you want to start investing to help your retirement fund, to make a side income, or even to replace your full income? The answer to this will help determine how you will behave when you get into the market.

There are many options that you can choose for goals when you want to invest. Choosing the right one can sometimes help you to figure out how much risk you want to take and which stocks you want to invest in. For example, if you are looking to turn the stock market investment into your full-time income, you may be willing to take on more risk to bring in more money. If you want to make just enough to put some in the bank or pay off a few bills, then it may be best to go with less risky options.

No matter which goal you choose for investing, you will quickly find that the stock market is one of the best options that you can choose for your investment. There are many companies that you can choose to work with, many strategies that work well, and even different levels of risk that you can pick from. You can pick a plan that has a bit more risk that will also help you earn more rewards, or you can take your time to learn more about the stock market and pick less risky options while still making money.

You do need to have a good idea of how the stock market works and how to get into the game before you start. First, we need to understand what a stock is. A stock is a type of security that will give the investor, or you if you choose this option, part ownership in the business that the stock belongs to. This also means that the investor will be able to claim some of the assets and earnings of the business as well. The buyer will be known as a shareholder, and along with some of the other investors, they will be the new owners of that business. The amount of ownership that you have will depend on a number of stocks that you possess. There are also two types of stocks including common stocks and preferred stocks.

How do I trade in stocks?

One of the first questions that you may have as a new investor is how to trade stocks. When you join in on the stock market, you must trade stocks using the stock exchange. This is simply the place where the sellers and buyers of stocks will come together and then agree on the price for a particular stock. There are a few places where you can physically go to do this, but for the most part, you will do your trades online.

Once you get into the stock market and look at it for a bit, you will notice that the prices of each stock will change all the time. Many different factors come into play when determining what the price of the stock will be. These factors change on a regular basis, which is what makes it so hard to keep the prices steady for the long term. For example, if the supply of the stock is pretty high while the demand is low, the price of that stock will stay lower. If the demand for the particular stock goes up and the supply goes down or stays the same, then the price of those stocks will go up as well. The prices of the various stocks will usually be what people in the stock market see as the worth of the stocks and can show how interested people are in purchasing that stock at one time or another.

Not only can you pay attention to the demand and supply of a particular stock, but you will also find that the earnings of the company behind the stock can determine how much it is worth as well. This means that you need to look at how much money the company is able to earn each year. Of course, the exact amount will change from one year to another, so it is a good place to start to see if the company is growing and if you will be able to make some money from the investment. It is easy to find these numbers by looking through some of the financial journals and reports that the company is required to put out in order to be on the stock market.

Keeping track of all the prices on the stock market can be hard, and the fact that there are a lot of reasons that these stock prices will change can be a hassle as well. You have to look at some of the changes that the company has recently made or will make soon. Addtionally, you need to look at how well the economy is doing at the time. What this all means is that you do need to do some research. Those who just jump right into the stock market and don't pay attention to what is going on around them are more likely to fail and lose a lot of money.

There is no rush when getting into the stock market. You can do this on your own time and do some thorough research to make sure you are picking out the right stocks and not just risking everything. Finding a good stockbroker to help you along the way can make the process so much easier as well.

Chapter 2: Picking Out Stocks to Invest In

After taking some time to research the stock market and what it has to offer, it is important that you take the time to pick out the right stocks. There are thousands of companies available on the stock market, but not all of them will provide you with a good return on investment. Some will provide you with one of the best opportunities to make money without all the risk and others will be failures right from the beginning. As a beginner, you may be worried about how you will sort these out so that you can pick the right stocks to make the most money for you.

The first thing that you should look at when you are ready to join the stock market is that you should never just pick out a stock, no matter what the circumstances are, simply because you heard through the grapevine or from a friend of a friend that the stock was a good one. Doing your own research is important. You can take the advice of other people, such as friends who are in the stock market and your broker, but remember that this is your investment and you need to be the one in control of it. Do some of your own research on the market, and you will soon learn which stocks are the best ones for your needs, regardless of what other people say.

If you have already done some research and have come up with a list of companies that you want to look at some more and possibly invest in, make sure to take some time searching on their website. Most of them will have information about their stocks, and this can be helpful when making your decision. You need to take a look at all of their reports on finances if possible to because this tells you how the company has done so far on the market. You will be surprised at how much information you are able to get about a company just by snooping around a little bit.

While there are a lot of things that you will need to consider when it comes to picking out a stock to work with, you need to go with one that will actually make you money in the process. Never pick a stock that is obviously going to cost you more than you can earn and try to go with the ones that are winners. There are a few things that you can take a look at to limit your risks including:

- The margin of profit for that company.
- The debts that a company has and how much those debts are.
- The return on equity with that company.
- The debt to equity ratio. This is a good thing to look up because it will give you an idea of how this particular company spends their money and whether they do so responsibly or not.
- How the company has done in the past and whether they are expected to do the same, better, or worse.

What should I be looking for?

So, you may be curious about what things you need to look for to pick out a good company to invest in. You will want to spend some time looking through charts and graphs to see how a particular stock has been doing inside the stock market, but that is only one part of the story. You also need to take a look at the company itself to see if it will maintain that status for the long term. For example, there may be a company who looks good when you go through the charts and graphs, but if they are not good at spending money or keeping their debts down, then they are not the company for you. Some of the different things that you should consider looking at when you are ready to pick out a stock includes:

Who manages the business

This is one of the first things that you should look at when you want to start investing in a company. Who manages the business will help you to figure out how the company is doing now as well as how it will do in the future. Many beginners consider the management of a company not all that important. However, if the current management is not doing well with running the company, even a solid company can go downhill fast.

Now, you need to carefully consider the management of a company before you decide to invest in it. There are a few points that you can consider such as what the return on equity is if the shareholders are still earning a profit each year. If the equity return of the company is five percent or higher, it is usually a safe bet that the company will keep growing and doing well. Also, look and see how the management is doing with others and with each other. Are they getting along and making decisions that are good for the company, or is there are a lot of internal fighting that could ruin the company?

Pick a sector that is doing well

When you are picking out stocks, it is important that you find some that come from a business sector that is also doing well. Depending on how the economy is doing, it is possible that some industries will still do well in a downturn, or at least some industries will do better than the rest. There are also times when the economy is doing well, but one or two industries are not doing as well as the rest of the market.

This is why it is so important to pick out industries that are doing well. You may also want to consider spreading your money out a bit so that you can avoid trouble if one of your industries starts to do poorly. And, while it is best to go with industries that are predicted to do well over a long period of time, if you find that one of your industries is not performing the way that you want, it is easy to sell that stock and try something else.

Growing profits
You also need to look for a company that is making profits. If you see a company that is losing money from the start, then it will be hard for you to get a good return on investment. You also want to make sure that the company

is getting bigger profits each year. When the company keeps on growing their profits, it is doing well and has a lot of popularity that is growing as well. This makes it a good investment option for many people. The bigger the profits, the better return on investment you will be able to get.

The size of your company

Some investors want to work with a company that is a little bit smaller. They think that these are easier to work with and that they will be able to monitor that company a little bit better than some of the bigger companies. However, there have been some studies done that show how smaller companies will actually carry more risks with them compared to investing in some of the bigger companies.

The reason for this is that a lot of the bigger companies have taken their time to become established. They didn't become big overnight, so you know that they will be safe investments. As a beginner who has never worked in the stock market, it is usually better to go with a company that is bigger and more established. After you have learned how to work in the stock market and you understand the types of risks that you want to take, you can choose to go with a smaller company if you would like.

Also, as a beginner, you should make sure that you are avoiding penny stocks. These sometimes are tempting because they are usually really inexpensive to work with. However, these companies are really risky and often they do not need to provide users and investors with financial information even though they are on the exchange. It is likely that you will lose a lot of money if you choose to work with these penny stocks. It is a better idea to stick with one of the main companies that are on the stock market so that you know they are safer options and you are more likely to make money.

Look at the dividend payments

When you look at a company, check and see if they are able to pay out dividends to their investors. Companies that are able to share their profits already are great options for a beginner to work with. This shows that the company is already able to manage their debts while still sharing the profits with the shareholders. It is likely that they will be able to do it again and you will continue to receive these payments in the future.

Also, when you are deciding how much you can make with dividend payments, you should go with a company that is able to pay you at least two percent. This is a good sign that the company is pretty steady and that you will be able to make a decent amount of money each year. If you can find one that is higher than the two percent, then you are able to make even more in profits.

Manageable debt

While you are taking a look at some of these companies to invest in, you should take a look at the debts that they have. The company doesn't necessarily need to be completely debt free, but they need to have a good balance between the amount of debt that they take on and the amount of profit that they are able to bring out.

There are some good debts that a company will have, especially if they are just starting out or if they have recently undergone an expansion. They may have some debts for their buildings, for their equipment and so much more. You are not likely to find a company that doesn't have any debt, but you should look for one that has kept their debt manageable for the profits that they make each year. If you are looking for a company and they have so much debt that they are barely able to cover it each month, then it is best to go with someone else. In this case, it is unlikely that they will be able to keep managing that debt and you will lose money.

Go with liquid stocks

And finally, another thing that you can consider when you are looking at stocks to invest in is how liquid those stocks are. Liquid stocks are good because these are the ones that you will easily be able to find sellers and buyers for. If you go with a stock that is not liquid, you may find that it is really hard to sell that stock later on when you want to leave the market. Most stocks will have some kind of liquidity with them, but the more liquid the stock is considered, the easier it is for you to sell it when you would like.

Try to find a stock that has a happy medium. You want it to be at a good price, so you do not want the demand for that stock to be too high. If the demand is too high, it will be too expensive to get ahold of it to start. But the demand needs to be high enough that when you are ready to leave the market, no matter what that reason is, you will be able to find someone who is willing to purchase the stocks from you.

There are a lot of things that you will need to consider when it comes to picking out the right stocks for your needs. You should do your research to figure out who is managing the company, how they are doing with their profits and their debts, and find stocks that will be easy to sell if you decide to leave the market. When you are able to do this, you are sure to find some good and secure stocks that will help you to make a good profit.

Chapter 3: How to Purchase Stocks

Earlier, we took some time to explore the things that you should look at to find the perfect stocks to invest in. You want to make sure that you pick out stocks that will actually bring you money, ones that have good management, steady profits, and manageable debts so that you can make money. After you have done some research on the stock market, it is time to enter the market and actually purchase the stocks that you want to invest in. Let's take a look at how you enter the market by purchasing stocks.

Use a broker

Since you are a beginner and you have not had the opportunity to work in the stock market yet, it may be a good idea to work with a broker. The broker will help you make smart decisions when it comes to the stocks that you should invest in. Brokers spend their time learning how to work with the market, and they have been doing work in this industry for many years. They have a lot of experience and expertise that is needed to help you make good decisions. Beginners can really benefit from taking the advice from a broker they trust.

There are actually a few types of brokers that you can choose to work with and it will depend on how much you would like to spend on the broker and how much advice you will end up needing. The first broker that you can work with is a full-service broker. This type of broker will be responsible for managing all of the stocks and purchases that happen on your account. You will be able to consult with them about any purchases that you are considering and the best steps that you can take to grow your portfolio. You can give some instructions and provide your opinion, but they will take over most of the work for your investment for you. If you have no idea what you are doing and you would like someone to hold your hand, the full-service broker is a good option for you.

Another option for brokers is to work with what is known as a discount broker. These brokers will cost you less than a full-service broker, but remember that it also means you will receive fewer services from them. You must put in more time and effort to get your investments done. However, they will help you to save some money and can really assist you to get some of the advice that you need in the investment world.

Consider a reinvestment plan

You can, while you are working on which stocks to go with, decide to work with one individual company. When you work with this company, you can take the profits that you earn through dividends, and then use that money to purchase more stocks through the same company. As you are first getting started, you will find that you may not be able to invest much, which will limit how many stocks you are able to purchase. When you take that money and reinvest it to get more stocks, rather than taking and personally using the money for your own reasons, can help you to get more profit in the future because you will own more stocks. Over time, your money will start to grow more, and it can help to reduce your risk of investing all at the same time.

Direct investing plans

Since you are a new investor, you will be able to choose whether you would like to work with a direct investment plan. With this kind of investment, you would not have to use a broker to make your purchases, which will save you some fees that you would spend on that person. For this one, you will choose to work directly with the individual company that you want to invest in. You will not go through the stock exchange, but rather, you will go through the company directly to purchase your stocks. There will be a few extra fees that will come with using this option, but they are smaller than what you will find with a broker, so it is a good way to save some money.

This one can be considered similar to the last option, but you will still be able to keep the dividends when you are done, rather than reinvesting those profits. You could choose to use that money to purchase more stocks, but it is not necessary to be considered a direct investment plan. You may want to work with this option if you feel like working with only one company and you don't think that working with a broker is necessary.

All of these options will help you to get your foot in the door of the stock market so that you can start to invest and earn a profit. Remember that in the beginning, you will probably only make a little bit of money, and you may even need to bring in a broker to do the work for you if you are confused, but the point is that you get started and find the option that works the best for you. Take a look through some of the options above and find the one that is sure to fit your style and give you the profits that you want.

Chapter 4: What Options Do I Have For Stock Market Investing?

There are quite a few options that you will be able to choose when you are ready to invest in the stock market. You will need to learn how to narrow down the niche and the industry that you want to work in to make things a little bit easier. While it is important to diversify your portfolio at some point, it is best for a new investor to keep things small.

The strategy that you choose to help you start investing will depend on a number of factors. Sometimes it depends on the money that you have to start with and how much you want to make. Sometimes it depends on the amount of risk involved or the research that you have done on the topic. But even when you have a good plan with lots of research, there are reasons why you should be skeptical and take your time with everything. In this chapter, we will talk about some of the options and even some of the niches that you can choose to help you invest in the right stocks for you.

Dividend Stocks

The first strategy that you can choose is to work with dividend stocks, and it works the best if you would like to pick out a long-term investment. Dividend stocks may not make you rich overnight, but it will help you to earn a lot of money consistently over many years. When going with dividend stocks, you want to make sure that you are picking stocks from companies that are doing well now and are projected to do well in the future. There are quite a few companies who will work out well for this, and if you pick the right one, you will be able to enjoy a percentage of the profits from that company each quarter for as long as you hold the stocks.

Now, it is important to realize that not all stocks that are available on the exchange will work with dividends. This means that you need to check with each company before deciding to use them for this process. Screening companies is a good idea as well because this will help you to figure out which companies will actually give you a dividend each quarter (if the company doesn't make a profit, they are not able to provide their shareholders with any dividends). Each company that trades on the stock exchange will need to put out financial statements. Make sure to utilize these to help you make good decisions.

As you go through your research, you should be able to come up with a list of companies that pay their shareholders a decent dividend. But you do not want to start out with too many companies, so it is now time to narrow the list down a little bit to find those that meet all your criteria. Some of the things that you should look into with each company that you are interested in will include:

- Look to see if the company has had a steady history of paying out their dividends. It is not a good thing if there is a lot of missed dividend

payments because this could show that there are some major issues with the company. It is best to go through their history as far as possible to see how consistent the dividend payments are.
- The next thing to look for is how high the return on equity is for this company. To make sure that you are picking out a good company, you need to look over the past five years and see a return on equity of at least fifteen percent if not higher.
- Each share that you are considering needs to have rising earnings and sales over time. If the shares are going down, then you know that you will lose money if you go with this stock.
- The dividends that are provided to the shareholders need to grow as well. This means that you will earn more money over time, instead of getting the exact same amount every year. A good company will see a growth in their dividends of at least five percent over ten years.

Take a look at the list of companies that you are interested in and check to see if they meet some of the requirements above. If they do, then they are a great option to go with, and you should consider investing your money in them.

Foreign stock investing

Another option that you can choose to go with is the foreign stock investing. This is an option that most beginners do not stick with because it is hard to follow what is going on in a foreign market. This means that if you want to go into this type of market, you need to do some extra research and pay special attention to what is going on in other countries. If you do this process correctly, there are a lot of companies overseas that are promising and can bring in more money than you can get in your own country. However, it is important to realize that some risks come with working with foreign stock investing.

There are actually a few benefits that you can enjoy when it comes to investing in foreign stocks. Some of the benefits that you will enjoy with these stock options include:

- The stocks that are available in foreign markets will provide you with some new investment opportunities. Based on your goals for investing, it sometimes is a little hard to find a company that you want to invest in, especially if you limit yourself to your own country. You may find that it is easier to find the right investments when you look in other markets.
- Foreign stocks can be a good option for those who are looking for new ways to diversify their portfolios. This can help you to spread out some of your risks, so consider investing your money into a variety of companies, even if you are looking at foreign markets.

While these benefits are really tempting for a beginner who wants to find lucrative companies to invest in, it is important to remember that working in a foreign market actually provides a much higher risk than working in the stock exchange in your market. Even if the company looks like a good and safe investment, it is important to take into account the exchange rate. Depending on which market you go into and the amount of dividend that you expect to make, the cost of exchanging the currency over to USD may take all your profits, which makes the risk of investing in these markets higher than before.

The market conditions are often going to be very different in another country compared to what is going on in your country. For example, the United States may be seeing an upturn in their economy while other countries deal with economies that are shaky. It does not matter what is going on in your home country; what matters is what is going on in whatever country you would like to invest in. This can be good news if the economy in your home country is doing poorly, but it is still something to be aware of.

While there is a lot of potential to make a high profit when you decide to invest in a foreign market, it is very risky, and that is why a lot of beginners choose to not go with this option at all. It may be a good idea to find a good broker and get some help if you decide to go with this as your investment option.

Penny stocks

Penny stocks are an option for investing that some people like to work with, but you have to realize that these are really risky. Beginners like these stocks because they are less expensive than some of the bigger names that are on the stock exchange. If you do not have a lot of money to get started with for this investment, the penny stocks can be a good option for you to go with because you may be better able to afford them.

It is important to realize that not all the companies on the penny stock exchange are reputable. These companies do not need to disclose financial information, and they do not need to meet the same requirements thatcompanies on the stock exchange need to. While there are some companies who will sell shares on this exchange to help them out while they are trying to meet the requirements of the stock exchange (and these are often really good companies to consider because their prices will go up), there are also a lot of failing companies that are working as penny stocks.

This can make it hard to know who you should work with. These penny stocks are really risky, and it is not always the best idea for a beginner to get into this market. Sometimes the value of the stock is hard to figure out, and even a little bit of negative movement can cause a big impact on your investment. Many times these companies are able to hide information from you, and you can lose out your whole investment in no time. These stocks are really volatile as well, which makes it harder to watch the market and make good decisions.

If you are a beginner and you are interested in checking out penny stocks and learning how they work, then you need to be careful and fully aware of all the risks that come with it. Some of the guidelines that you can consider following when you want to get into penny stocks and still see a return on your investment include:

- Pay attention to some of the warnings that you see.

There are some regulators on this market, and if they are sending out some warnings about a particular company, it is worth your time to pay attention.

- Don't always believe what you see. These companies are not held up to the same standards as companies on the stock exchange are. Do your own research and learn as much about the company as possible.
- Learn some more about how penny stocks work. We talked briefly about them, but it is so important to take a look at these stocks and learn more about them before you enter the market.
- Some companies will offer penny stocks, but they are not going to provide you with a lot of information. The less information that is present in a company, the bigger the risk there is to invest in them. Double check that a company is as honest as possible with their information, especially financial information, before you decide to invest.

These are some of the main options that you can work with when you are ready to invest your money in the stock market. Make sure to look through each category and decide which one is the best for your needs.

Chapter 5: Picking Out Your Investment Strategy

Now that we have spent some time looking at all the different options that you have available when picking out a stock, it is time to pick out the strategy that you want to use when it is time to invest in the stock market. There are various strategies that you can work with, and all of them can help you to earn money. The biggest issue with the investment strategy is that you need to fully understand how it works. If you don't understand the strategy or you keep mixing it up with other ones, you will not see success.

So, the first thing that we need to do here is to learn a bit more about the different investment strategies that you can choose from. There are a lot of options, but you must understand how they work if you want any hope for success. Let's take a look at some of the most popular investment strategies and how they should work.

Working with the fundamental analysis

The first investment strategy that we will look at is called a fundamental analysis. This is an easy option to work with, but it does take some time, and you will need to bring out some of your research skills. The goal of working with this kind of analysis is that you want to look at the company that you want to invest in and then figure out what the intrinsic value of that company is. This means that you want to figure out how much the stock of that company is worth when compared to the current value that the company has on the stock exchange.

If the intrinsic value of that company is already higher than what the company is currently trading for, it is a good idea to make a purchase of that stock. When this happens, it means that there is a high likelihood that the stock will go up in price in the near future and you will make money if you enter into the trade at the right time.

Next on the list to figure out is which method you would like to use to help you figure out the intrinsic value of our chosen company. There may be some similarities between these methods, but it is important to pick one. First, you could start out by taking a look at the sum of the discounted cash flows for that company. What this means is that the company will be worth all its future profits when you add them together. Then you can take these projected future profits and discount them so that you can account for what is known as time value, or the force that says that $1 today will be worthless when you get to the future because of inflation.

The idea of the intrinsic value of the company being equal to the future profit will help you to understand how a company can provide more value to its owners. Think about owning your own business and how its worth will include all the money that you can take in as profit when you get to the end of the year. This is only going to be possible if you make a profit after you pay your debts, salaries, suppliers, and other bills first and then have some money left over. This is what you want to find when you look at a company to invest in.

So, where are you going to find some of these numbers? You should be able to find these directly from the company and their financial reports. These reports are required before the company is able to join the stock exchange, which makes it easy for you to take a look through them. You should also take some time to dig deeper and look at the news about a particular company to figure out what numbers are being announced to the public. When you are able to bring all of this information together, it is much easier to help you go through this analysis and pick out the companies that are best for you.

Value investing

Another option or strategy that you can go with when you are ready to invest in the stock market is called value investing. This is actually a really popular strategy that you can try out because it is so successful. When you work with value investing, you will go with a company that has really strong fundamentals, such as strong book value, cash flow, dividends, and earnings. You will then take all that information and compare it to what the stocks are selling for on the market.

When you are a value investor, you will need to look for companies which are undervalued on the market, no matter what the reason, compared to their fundamentals. When a company is undervalued, it means that you are able to purchase their stocks for a great price. As long as the fundamentals of that company are strong, it is very likely that the price of those stocks will increase to their market value, and sometimes higher, once everyone else catches on. You can make a lot of good money with this option as long as you pick a company that fits the bill and you get on it quickly.

Now, it is important to realize that there is a difference between a junk stock and one that is undervalued. If you go with the junk stocks just because they are lower in price, you will end up in some trouble. When you are looking through the market, there are always some companies who will have lower-priced stocks. This is not because those companies are undervalued, but because these companies are just not worth all that much. These companies could have some other issues with them, such as high debt to profit ratio, bad management, or some other reason that they are not worth much.

When you are looking at value stocks, you are looking at companies that actually have good dividends, low debt, and a strong earning potential. Often there is something in the market that is working against them, and so the value of the stock is discounted temporarily. If this is true about the company, then it is likely that their value will go up in no time.

Some beginners do not like to work with value investing. They may feel that most stocks will be at the price where they should be and that it does not matter what the fundamentals are. They may figure that if a stock is supposed to be ranked at a higher price, then it would be at that higher price. There are some investors, on the other hand, who like this method because it helps them to find some good stock investments without having to jump in too late in the game.

CAN SLIM

You can also try using a strategy that goes under the acronym of CAN SLIM. This one will take on a few extra steps to help you see success, but it may be just what a beginner needs to ensure that they are doing the proper research before picking out a new stock to invest in. Let's take a look at what all of these parts mean and how they can help you to pick out a good stock to invest in.

C = Current earnings

With this part, you need to look at the company and see how much they are earning now in the present. You can look at the most recent quarter of the company and then see how it compares to what was made in that same quarter the year before. If this is a solid company, then you should notice that the profits went up from one year to the next. If the profits went down, the company could be experiencing some issues that you want to avoid. It is a good idea to see a growth of twenty percent or more to ensure that you have less risk in the investment.

A = Annual earnings

Now, we will take a look at how much earnings for the company have grown over the past year. You should not just look over one year, though. It is best to look through at least the past five years, if not more, of that company. When you are looking through these five years, you should see that each year has at least a little bit of growth. It is ideal if the growth over the full five years is about twenty-five percent if not more.

N = New

You can also take a look at the company and then find out if some new changes occurred within the company. There are a lot of changes that a business can go through - some will harm the company, and others are good for the company. If you see that some of the harmful changes are being implemented, it is best to leave that organization behind. But if there are some changes in a product being released or within management, it could increase the value of the corporation in the near future.

S = supply and demand

For this criteria, you must take a look at how the supply and the demand of that company is doing. This helps you to know how much the price of the stock is likely to go up in the future. If all things are considered equal in the market, it is easier for some of the smaller firms, who will have fewer shares, to show more gains compared to the bigger ones. The reason for this is because the larger companies will need to deal with a higher demand than some smaller companies just to get it to show up as gains at all.

L = Leader

Here we will take a look at the leaders and the laggards in the market and see how these are able to change your decisions. No matter which industry you will work in, there will be some companies who are considered the leaders. These are the ones that will provide the best dividends to their shareholders. Conversely, there are a few companies who will be lagging behind in the industry, and they are not able to provide a good return on investment to their shareholders. Make sure that you are picking out a company that will be one of the leaders if you would like to make the most money possible.

I = Institutional Sponsorship

The reason that you want to work with institutional sponsorship is because you will be able to see that the company is popular. If you are looking for a company and it doesn't have this kind of sponsorship at all, this means that many money managers have decided not to use this company and there is usually a big red flag reason why they didn't. It is best to pick out a company that has a minimum of three of these institutional owners.

You do need to be watchful if a company has too many of these institutions involved in the process. There is such a thing as a company being owned too much by institutions, and when this happens, it means it is too late for you to get into this company. If you do get into the company, you will probably lose out when those institutions decide to sell the company off. You want a few money managers to be involved, but not too many that it all becomes too congested.

M = Market direction

And the final thing that you will take a look at is the market direction. Any time that you wish to look at a new stock, it is important to look through the market conditions and figure out whether you are dealing with a bear or a bull market. If you do not understand where the market is heading, this will cause a big amount of risk to your gains, and it will be much easier to make some bad decisions on your investment.

Income investing

Another option that you can choose when you are picking out an investment strategy is known as income investing. With income investing, you need to look over the company and then decide whether they are able to provide you with a fairly steady stream of income. This is an easier method, and many beginners like to work with it. When you think about the investment as a way to make a steady income, instead of a way to make money quickly, it is easier to pick out less risky options. There are a variety of options that you would be able to work with for this, such as bonds and fixed income security. There are a number of stocks that can also do this as long as you pick the right one.

To make the income investment work for you, you must be careful that you pick out stocks that will provide a dividend that will be around for a long time. Remember that the average yield for most dividend stocks will be somewhere around three percent. But if you are looking to use this dividend as a way to make an income, then you need to go with a stock that can provide you with a profit of six percent, if not higher, or you are wasting your time.

Of course, in addition to looking through the market and picking out the stocks that will provide you with a steady income stream, you also need to read through the policies that the company releases about the dividends. This can be important because some companies will not keep handing out the dividends in the future. You can also look through this information to see whether the company added some more dividends as this will affect your profits as well. For example, if you see that the company increased their dividend plans by quite a bit over the last year, this is usually an overly optimistic position, and it is best to go with another company to protect your investment.

Income investing is a long-term solution. This is not a method that you will join and then sell out quickly when the market turns on you. The whole point is to provide you with an income each quarter that you are able to use just like any other income that you bring in. The trick here is that you need to be able to find the companies who will be able to provide you with this kind of income.

Dogs of the Dow

Some beginner investors like to work with the strategy that is known as Dogs of the Dow. This is a simple approach that is meant to help you make your money over the long-term. If you are looking to chase the market around and hope to make money quickly, this is not going to be the right option for you. For this strategy, you will look at the

30 companies that have been listed in the DIJA or the Dow Jones Industrial Average. From here, you will pick out ten investments that are performing really well. After you have finished with that first year, you will take a look at the list again, and pick the ten that are doing well for the second year. This does require some readjusting to your portfolio but helps you to pick out companies that are always doing well.

Every few years or so, you may need to make some adjustments and get rid of some of the stocks that you own. You will replace them with new stocks that are now in the top of the DIJA to help you do well. This is hard to keep up with sometimes, but going off that list will make things so much easier.

With this strategy, just like when you pick out any of the other strategies that are on this list, Dogs of the Dow is not necessarily foolproof, and there are times when it is not going to provide you with the return on investment that you would like. Generally, though, it is a good way to find companies that are doing well and can provide you with a good return on investment. If you are a beginner and don't know how to work in the market, or you are worried about finding time to research the right companies to invest in, then this is the right option for you.

The reason that a lot of beginners choose to go with Dogs of the Dow is that
it is really simple to understand. You will be able to save a lot of time by not having to look through all those charts, and yet you will still be able to see some good results with

your investment. All that you need to do is set aside some time when a new year starts and look at this list. Then you go through and make the changes that are necessary to your portfolio so that everything matches up the right way. There are a few times that you will need to make changes to the stocks you are holding, but many of them will stay the same from year to year, so the work on this strategy is minimal.

There are many strategies that you are able to choose from when it comes to working in the stock market, and we have only brought up a few of the ones that you may be interested in. All of them can be successful as long as you follow them correctly. Pick out the one that is the most comfortable for you and you will start to make a good return on investment in no time.

Chapter 6: Different Styles That Expert Traders Use for Stock Trading

It is also possible to get into the stock market and do what is known as stock trading. Stock trading is a little bit different because you are not focusing on the long-term with this option. Instead, you are focusing on how to make a profit more quickly in the stock market. You will try to purchase stocks when they are low, such as when the company is undervalued or right before the value of the company is expected to go up, and then you will sell them in the future for a profit. This can work well if you know how to read the market and you are willing to take the risk. Sometimes you will only hold onto your position for a day or less and other times you may hold this position for a few months, but it is never meant to be a long-term investment type, and you likely will not hold onto the stocks long enough to earn any dividends.

If you want to go with the option of stock trading, then it is imperative that you learn how to read the market and that you are willing to move fast. You may be able to purchase a stock at a discount or a very low price, and then you must sell it when that stock price goes up. The hardest part is to figure out when a stock is low because it is discounted or the market is low, or when a stock is low because the company is not worth much. If you pick a stock from one of the latter, then the price will never go up, and you will not make a profit.

If you are interested in giving stock trading a try, there are a few options that you can look into to get the most out of your money. As you learn how to use these strategies and get into the market for some time, you will be able to bring your own personal style into the mix as well. Let's take a look at some of these styles and see how they can help you become successful with stock trading.

Position trading

Some of the styles that you can do with stock trading will require you to get in and out of the market within a few days if not sooner. This can be a bit intense for a lot of beginners to the stock market, and you may not want to try that until you get more comfortable. Position trading is a good option if you would like to have some room when it comes to the trading period between purchasing and selling your stock. Many of these trades can last for a few months, and some for even longer.

The benefit of working with position trading is that you will be able to hold onto the stock for a little bit longer so you can watch the trends in the market before selling. If things go south, you will have more time to hold onto the stock and wait it out until the market goes up. There are a lot of sudden changes that can occur with a stock from day to day, even with a steadier stock, and this method will give you some room to breathe.

Of course, this one is more similar to stock market investing than some of the others because you are holding onto the stock for a longer period of time. However, you can choose to make it more of a short-term trade. Instead of holding onto the stocks for years, you may only hold onto the stock for a few weeks. As a position trader, it will become your job to look at weekly as well as monthly charts to help you make some good trading decisions. You will not really need to spend your time looking at short-term price changes with this strategy.

Day trading

Some traders want to work on a short-term investment inside the stock market. Day trading can be the answer to that because it is a fast-paced option that can be hard to keep up with. If you are not willing to constantly watch the market or you are not willing to take some risks, then day trading is not the option for you. As a day trader, it will be your job to purchase a stock sometime during the day, usually in the morning, and then you will need to sell that stock before the market closes on that same day. You are not allowed to keep your stocks longer than this so you will need to sell, regardless of whether you end up with a winning or losing position.

Day traders look at the market differently than the position trader will. They do not care how the stock will do over the long-term because they do not plan to hold that stock for more than a few hours. However, they are really interested in how the stock has been doing over the past few days. When they are able to see a good trend, they will be better able to make some predictions about what will happen with their stocks. This helps them to make some good purchasing decisions.

Day trading is not going to yield you a lot of money off each trade. No stock sees huge increases in prices in just a few hours. But if you do a lot of little trades throughout the week, you will be able to make a good deal of profits from this trading method.

Swing trading

Swing trading is another option that you can choose to go with when you want to get into stock trading. With this trading style, you will purchase the stocks that you want to use, hold onto them for up to two weeks, and then sell them at a higher price. This is similar to day trading, but you will get up to a few weeks rather than just a few hours.

A swing trader will look at a stock and try to determine if that stock value will go up in the next few weeks. Perhaps they have been doing some research, and they see that a big announcement is about to come out concerning a company. That company's stocks may be pretty low at that moment, but because of a new expansion or a new product launch, the price of the stock may be expected to go up. The swing trader would purchase the stock when the price is low, hold onto it for a few weeks, and then sell to make a profit.

The fundamentals of a company are not going to matter as much with swing trading because you are not going to hold your position for all that long. The swing trader is just looking for companies that are likely to see an increase in the price and value of their stocks sometime in the near future. It doesn't really matter to them who runs the company or how much they pay out in dividends because the swing trader is not planning on being in the market that long.

Scalp trading

Some traders will choose to work in what is known as scalp trading. This can be considered similar to day trading, but you will be much busier with this option. Your goal as a scalp trader is to be constantly purchasing and selling your stocks non-stop throughout the day. The main agenda for the scalp trader is to focus on the day to day changes of the stock market because this will help them determine when to make a purchase and when to sell.

The scalper has the goal of purchasing a stock at a low price, and then they will sell it as soon as the price goes up. Since the market is constantly going up and down, this is possible as long as you are able to pay close attention to what is going on in the market. You often will only make a small amount on each sale, but if you do hundreds of these during the same day, it can quickly add up.

Picking your trading style

Above, you learned about some of the best trading styles that you can use if you would like to work with stock trading. Now that you have learned about them a little bit, it is time to pick out the one that you would like to use. But how are you going to make this kind of decision if you have never traded in the stock market? Some of the questions that you should ask yourself when picking out a new trading style include:

- How big is my account?
- How much risk am I willing to take to make a profit?
- What is my trading personality?
- Do I have any experience with trading or am I just getting started and need to work on something easier?
- How much time will I be able to devote to my trades? Position trading just needs to be checked on occasion while scalping and day trading will require you to spend a lot of time watching the market.

For most investors, the amount of risk that they are willing to take and the amount of time that they have available for trading will determine which trading style they choose to go with. It is not possible for everyone to give up all their time, at least in the beginning, to the trading method, but that is what options like scalping will require. Others may not be willing to take on that much risk just to get a little bit of profit. It is all going to depend on what you would like to get out of this investment and your own trading personality.

In the beginning, just pick out one style that you are willing to work with. In time, as you earn more money and get more experience with the stock market, you can start diversifying your portfolio a bit more and can add in more of these styles to the mix. This will help you to make a lot more money in the long-term, but it is best to start out slow as a beginner.

Chapter 7: Rules That Help to Reduce Your Risks When Investing in the Stock Market

As a beginner in the stock market, it is important that you learn some of the best ways to reduce your risk. The stock market can be a good way to make money, but many beginners will fall prey to some of the mistakes that make this a really big risk. There is enough risk in the investment on its own, so you need to find ways to reduce your risks to make as much money as possible. Some of the steps that you can take to ensure that you are getting the most out of your investment include:

Do not follow the crowd

When you decide to get into stock market investing, you must learn how to make decisions on your own. It is tempting to always listen to your broker or to listen to the friend who has been on the market for a long time. While it is just fine for you to take the advice of others when you are getting started, you must remember that this is your investment. No one else has money on the line when you pick a certain stock or go with a certain strategy - only you do.

What this means is that you can still ask for advice and suggestions from other people. Talking to your broker and some friends who may know the market a little bit better is fine. However, take everything with a grain of salt. You will run into troubles if you hear what someone else says and then jump right in without even thinking about the investment. Always do your own research and use your own judgment to figure out which investments are the best for you.

Pick out a strategy and always stick with it

As you should know by now, there are a lot of different strategies that you can work with when it is time to invest in the stock market. All of these strategies have the potential of making you money, but you need to make sure that you fully understand the strategy that you are working with. If you are not using the method in the proper way, you will not be able to make money.

You also need to make sure that when you pick a strategy, you are sticking with that strategy the whole time. It is easy for a beginner to see a new approach that they think is good, but then try to switch right in the middle of a trade because it is not going the way that they want. This is dangerous. You are never going to succeed when you are splitting up two strategies. There are times, no matter which strategy that you pick, where you are not going to make money, and that is okay. You should just leave the market and call it good, rather than losing more money because you tried to switch your game plan.

You may be tempted to switch out your strategy because you do not fully understand how to manage itor because you start losing money. However, the second that you try to switch during a trade, the harder it will be to make money and keep your investment safe. You can always switch out strategies when the trade is done if you do not like using the one you picked, but stick it out until the trade is done.

Forget about the timing

Timing the market is never a good idea. There are a lot of beginners who will try to figure out how to time the stock market, but they often end up losing a lot of money rather than earning anything. Experts in all industries agree that it is pretty much impossible to find the exact tops and exact bottoms of a stock, and if you happen to reach them, it was because you are lucky, not because of good planning.

The issue here is that you can't predict how other people will react to a market. You can make some good guesses, but it is impossible to tell for certain when people will start selling or buying a particular stock. If you are trying to buy at the exact lowest point and then sell at the exact highest point, you will miss out on a lot of great opportunities. What you need to focus on instead is finding when the stock is at a good discount for your purchase and then selling the stock when it gets above its market value. This may not give you maximum profit, but you will earn a profit, and it helps you to avoid staying in the market too long.

Some financial advisors insist that timing the market is the only way that you can make a good profit in the stock market. The issue with this is that this strategy is often going to backfire on you. Additionally, while it affects you quite a bit, it will have no effect on the advisor. If you spend too much of your time trying to outsmart the market, you will be the one who loses.

Only invest what you can afford

When you see a good investment opportunity, it is tempting to jump in and use all the money that you have. You may go out and use all your savings and some of the money from your paychecks this month in the hopes that it will turn out well and you will become rich. But what happens if the investment doesn't go the way that you plan? Now you have nothing, and you may not even be able to pay your bills the next month.

One of the best practices that you can do when you get started with stock investing is that you only invest the money that you would be comfortable with losing. No one wants to lose money on an investment, but it is something that can happen. If you go into the market assuming that you will never lose, you are setting yourself up for a lot of trouble. Perhaps you should consider setting up a savings account ahead of time and putting some money in to help you with your investments without worrying that you are investing too much. No matter which method you choose to go with, make sure that you only add in the amount of money to the investment that wouldn't be disastrous if you end up losing.

Keep your expectations realistic

There are a lot of beginners who will join the stock market

and hope that they are able to make a lot of money. They may hear that it is possible to lose money in this market, but they figure that they can outsmart the market and that they will not end up losing all that much in the process. However, this is a bad way to enter the market. Even seasoned stock market investors who have been doing this for years will still lose money. There are many times when the market does something that you do not expect, and you can lose money no matter how much you plan.

In addition, going into the market and thinking you will earn money overnight is a bad idea. Some investments could potentially make you rich, but these are really risky. It is unlikely that you will actually succeed because the risk is so high, and you will most likely lose more money than you can afford to lose.

Going into the stock market is risky enough. Do not make it worse by going into the market with expectations that are not all that realistic. Understand that you can make some money in this investment, but it will often take some time to see that success. You must also understand that there are some times, no matter how hard you plan ahead, when you will end up losing money in the process.

Keep the emotions out of the game

You also need to make sure that you are able to keep emotions out of the game. As soon as those emotions come into play, you will start losing money. These emotions will often lead you to make poor decisions, and you are more likely to lose out on your investment.

This is why having a good strategy in place will make all the difference when it comes to making money with the stock market. This strategy will set up all the rules that you need to follow. It will tell you when to enter the market when you should leave the market, and all the steps in between. It basically outlines what you need to do, taking most of the decisions out of the game and allowing you to keep your emotions away as well.

One thing that you must learn to avoid at all costs is revenge trading. This starts when you end up losing some money on one trade because you made bad decisions or the market did not react the way that you wanted. Instead of just taking the loss and learning from it, you decide that you need to start making that money back right away. You go into risky investment options in the hopes of earning that money back quickly. Often investors who choose to go with revenge trading will not think through their decisions. The only thinking that they do is that they want to earn the money back. They will pick bad investments and not listen to the advice of others along the way. Because of this, they often lose a ton more money than they would have if they just learned from the mistake and moved on.

If you are someone who is really emotional or can let their decisions be affected by what is going on around them, or if you are worried about losing money in the process of trading, then investing in the stock market may not be the right choice. There are times when the market will not behave the way that you want, and there isn't much you can do about it. For these kinds of people, there are a lot of other investments, including ones that are less risky, that can help you earn good money as well.

Set your stop points

Another thing that you can consider doing is to set up some stop points. These are basically the points when you will exit the market, both when you are making profits and when you are losing. These can help to minimize your risks because you will make the decisions about these stop points before you enter the market and money is at stake. If you forget to do these, it can sometimes be hard to get out of the market at the right time, no matter how much logic you use.

The first stop point that you need to set is the one where you will exit the market when you are losing money. While you never want to think about losing money, it is much better to do this before you put any money in. This stop point should be at a place where you would still be comfortable with losing that money if things go wrong. Then, as soon as the market reaches that point, you will exit the market, no matter what may happen later on.

Some beginners find that it is tempting to stay in the market, even when they are losing money. They figure that the market will return and that they will be able to recoup their losses if they just stay in. This rarely ever works, and if you keep in the market, you are likely to keep losing money. With this stop point, you can keep your losses to a minimum and re-enter the market later on if you decide to.

You should also consider adding in a stop point to exit when you have made enough profits. Yes, it would be nice to plan for unlimited profits, but this is not going to happen, no matter which industry you choose to invest in. Adding this stop point in will ensure that you get some profit. Without it, you may be tempted to stay in the market too long, and when the market turns, you may end up losing all that profit and more.

It is best to set up these stop points ahead of time for each trade before you invest any money into the market. This will ensure that you are making logical decisions, long before the emotions can come into play, and you will be surprised at what a difference it can make in the amount of profit that you enjoy with this investment.

As a beginner in the stock market, there are a lot of things that you need to consider. You have to understand how the market works, which stocks to pick, when to get into and out of the market, and so much more. However, if you follow the tips and tricks in this guidebook and stick to the rules in this chapter, you will see the amazing results that you want.

Conclusion

Thank you for making it through to the end of this book! Let's hope it was informative and able to provide you with all of the tools you need to achieve your goals - whatever they may be.

The next step is to take a look at which investment strategy you would like to use when it comes to working with stock market investing. There are many different investment opportunities that you can go with, but the stock market provides the most variety, and the most fun, when it comes to putting your money to work for you.

Finally, if you found this book useful in any way, a review on Amazon is always appreciated!

Cryptocurrency

The Complete Beginner's Guide to Investing and Trading in Cryptocurrencies

© Copyright 2018 by John James - All rights reserved.

The following eBook is reproduced below, with the goal of providing information that is as accurate and reliable as possible. Regardless, purchasing this eBook can be seen as consent to the fact that both the publisher and the author of this book are in no way experts on the topics discussed within, and that any recommendations or suggestions that are made herein are for entertainment purposes only. Professionals should be consulted as needed prior to undertaking any of the actions endorsed herein.

This declaration is deemed fair and valid by both the American Bar Association and the Committee of Publishers Association and is legally binding throughout the United States.

Furthermore, the transmission, duplication or reproduction of any of the following work including specific information will be considered an illegal act, irrespective of if it is done electronically or in print. This extends to creating a secondary or tertiary copy of the work or a recorded copy and is only allowed with an express written consent of the Publisher. All additional rights reserved.

The information in the following pages are broadly considered to be a truthful and accurate account of facts, and as such any inattention, use or misuse of the information in question by the reader will render any resulting actions solely under their purview. There are no scenarios in which the publisher or the original author of this work can be in any fashion deemed liable for any

hardship or damages that may befall them after undertaking information described herein.

Additionally, the information in the following pages is intended only for informational purposes and should thus be thought of as universal. As befitting its nature, it is presented without assurance regarding its prolonged validity or interim quality. Trademarks that are mentioned are done without written consent and can in no way be considered an endorsement from the trademark holder.

Introduction

Cryptocurrencies are the hottest craze in the financial world right now, with everyone wanting to learn more about them and find out how they can invest in these unique currency forms. The craze really sprung when Bitcoin was introduced in 2009 and soared over the years to the point where now, at the time of writing this, it is narrowing in on a value of $13,000 USD. With people realizing how incredible the returns can be on these investments, everyone is interested in finding how they can get their piece of the pie. The great thing is, this further increases the value of many of these currencies as the supply and demand balance leads more toward the demand than the supply.

If you have ever wondered how you can get involved in cryptocurrencies, then this book is perfect for you. "*Cryptocurrency*: The Complete Beginner's Guide to Investing and Trading in Cryptocurrencies" will answer any questions you might have about getting started in this lucrative investment opportunity. You will learn about exactly what a cryptocurrency is, how they came about, and what made them so popular. You will also learn about many of the most popular cryptocurrencies available on the market today and what makes them unique from other cryptocurrencies that are presently available. You will also learn about how to buy and sell, and store your cryptocurrencies. Finally, you will be given some of the best advice on how to truly get good at this investment practice so that you can make the most back from it.

Cryptocurrency investing can seem intimidating, especially

if you are not overly familiar with the world of finances and cryptocurrencies themselves. However, it is actually extremely simple to get started and, with the right moves, you could end up earning incredible returns on your initial investments. The real key is in educating yourself and researching as much as possible so that you can make sound judgment calls and maximize your returns. You have come to the perfect place to acquire all of that information, too.

While this book will not go excessively into detail on each specific cryptocurrency available to you, it will help you get started and increase your confidence in this trading and investing strategy. You will also be guided towards how you can maximize your knowledge and increase your understanding so that you can make the most educated decisions on every investment you make.

If you are ready to begin tackling the world of cryptocurrency trading and investing, let's begin!

Chapter 1: What Are Cryptocurrencies?

When people think of cryptocurrency, most often the first thought in their mind is about Bitcoin. This popular cryptocurrency was the pioneer of digital currencies and has continued to dominate mainstream headlines everywhere. If you have already done some investigating into the world of cryptocurrencies, then you likely already know that there are many different currencies available to you nowadays. However, if this is your first time really digging deep, then you may be unaware that there are actually several different coins that you can use in addition to bitcoin in the modern cryptocurrency world.

Before we really get into the different kinds of cryptocurrency, however, why don't we take some time to understand what cryptocurrency actually is. This will give you the opportunity to have a clear understanding of what this type of currency is and why so many people are eager to invest in it. As well, when it comes to investing, you should always be clear on what it is exactly that you are investing in to prevent yourself from making a poor decision that results in you losing out on funds. So, before we get much further, let's explore what a cryptocurrency really is.

What is A Cryptocurrency?

Put simply, a cryptocurrency is a form of digital currency that is created, bought, sold, traded, and used all in the digital realm. There is no material object associated with the currency. Unlike traditional currencies which can be physically held through bills, coins, and other physical goods, cryptocurrencies are strictly dealt with on computers.

The concept for cryptocurrencies has been around for a long time. Back in the nineties, many different groups of people came together to try and design a cryptocurrency that would be successful and take away the need for traditional currencies. However, all of these attempts failed for one reason or another. In 2009, however, Bitcoin emerged. This cryptocurrency was the first successful one to ever hit the market, and even then it started out somewhat slow and with a great deal of concern and disbelief from the public. The creator, who goes by the alias Satoshi Nakamoto, was able to successfully design a coin that lived up to all of the initial desires and expectations of cryptocurrency. To this day, Bitcoin is still one of the most popular and widely traded cryptocurrencies. However, it is quickly finding itself amongst competition in recent years as new forms of cryptocurrencies are constantly emerging.

Cryptocurrency is built on a peer-to-peer network system. This means that there are no banks, financial institutions, or other third-parties involved with transactions that are conducted through cryptocurrencies. Instead, they are made through complex computer algorithms and then owned/traded by the owners themselves. There is no need to worry about banking fees, transaction fees, or any other fees as the currencies are not actually owned by anyone other than the holder of the currency itself.

Cryptocurrency is an incredible concept and is rapidly evolving into an incredible reality, too. This does not mean that it comes without faults, however. There are still many things that are being sorted out and understood by those who are responsible for creating the algorithms and facilitating the trades. For example, to facilitate payments and transactions, you need to use a payment network. One major problem that these networks used to face was the issue with double-spending. This is the practice of spending the same amount twice, and it can happen through loopholes in the system. Although this is an issue, it is not something that most people worry about. That is because, in modern cryptocurrencies, these networks use a decentralized system to keep records of balances. This means there are several servers responsible for keeping a record of transactions. If anyone were to try and alter the information within these servers to double-spend their cash, it would immediately be declined. No record of the attempted transaction would even be stored because it would be considered an illegitimate transaction and therefore it would simply be shut down.

This is the exact reason why cryptocurrencies failed for so long. Many of the developers were attempting to create a cryptocurrency that was based on a centralized server. This meant that a single server was responsible for the information stored around transactions. A simple hack into the system could result in the currency being double-spent as one could override the computer itself. However, Nakamoto managed to create and introduce a de-centralized server that created the same system we just discussed. As a result, the issue of double-spending is no longer a major issue with modern cryptocurrencies.

Upon realizing this, creating the de-centralized server system, and then launching Bitcoin, Nakamoto brought an entirely new era of possibility to cryptocurrencies. Now, all of the cryptocurrencies that have followed Bitcoin are built much in the same way, resulting in the process being far more secure for everyone involved.

But What are they, Really?

You now have a general idea of what cryptocurrencies are: a digital form of currency that can be used in place of traditional currencies. However, you may still be wondering about what they are *exactly*. As in, what exactly does a digital currency look like? How does it have any value? How does a server know that one even exists, to begin with? Let's look deeper into this so that you can understand the inner workings of cryptocurrencies and why they are a "thing" rather than just an illusion that someone made up.

Like traditional currencies, cryptocurrencies have a basis. There is a "thing" in existence that proves there is a form of currency there, to begin with. Someone did not just wake up one day, decide to formulate an imaginary currency and begin exchanging a theory or an illusion. There is an actual physical representation of these currencies, even though it doesn't exist in a materialistic way. Just because you cannot hold the currency in your physical wallet or in your hand does not mean that there is not some form of proof of its existence. In fact, its existence is very real and valid. Here's how.

Essentially, at the very basis of what a cryptocurrency is, it consists of limited entries in a database that cannot be changed without specific conditions being fulfilled. This may not sound overly fancy or specific, but it does fully embody exactly what a cryptocurrency is.

If you want to get a really solid understanding of what the cryptocurrency world actually looks like, consider your online banking through your traditional bank. When you put funds into your account, the physical money you own is taken away and turned into a digital number on a screen. Then, every time you use your bank card to make a purchase, money is deducted from your account to reflect the new balance. If money is put into your account, you can see it added to your balance. Essentially, it is a database that manages your money, and the value cannot be changed without a certain condition being fulfilled. Those conditions would include spending it which would reduce your balance, or being given money which would increase it.

The same is true for cryptocurrency. There is a decentralized database that recognizes these digital currency "entries." Each time you invest in or are paid in cryptocurrency, you are given a balance. If you spend it or sell it, your balance is reduced. At a very basic level, it is no different than using your bank balance on your debit card.

Why Does Cryptocurrency Matter?

The very fact that you are reading this book proves that cryptocurrency has sparked your interest. However, you may be wondering why people are so excited about it. What is so revolutionary about this new form of currency that people want to cultivate it and replace traditional currency with it? How can it truly be that different? The answer is simple: cryptocurrency is free of all of the limitations that are held by traditional currencies.

The biggest reason why cryptocurrencies matter is based on the transactional properties held by the cryptocurrencies. These currencies have features that do not exist in traditional currency transactions which make them more secure, easier to access, and ultimately focused in a "for the people" approach. This is based on the peer-to-peer networking system that the currencies are built on. There are five primary transaction-based properties that make these currencies so revolutionary from traditional currencies. They are outlined in the following points.

Irreversible. When it comes to traditional currencies, particularly those held on a bank card or credit card, transactions can be reversed. This can be a major issue for retailers. In fact, this issue is fairly prominent and takes place on a daily basis. It is a scam whereby someone requests a service or purchases a product from a retailer. They pay with a debit or credit card. Then, later, they call their banking company and claim that the transaction was false and that they never made that transaction. The bank then reverses the transaction, refunding the individual with their funds. Now, they have received free products or services because the transaction was reversed. There is not a lot that a company can do when this happens, either, despite it being recognized as a form of fraud.

With cryptocurrencies, the transactions are irreversible. Once the de-centralized server is in agreeance with the transaction, and it has been processed, there is no way to remove its existence from the system. You cannot reverse it or otherwise commit fraud by having the transaction "removed." These transactions are also hard to manipulate or fraudulently put through as both the merchant and the customer require their own unique keychains or digital passwords to validate the transaction. After both parties have inputted their transactions, they have given permission for the transaction to be conducted and there is no way to claim otherwise. Since no one else has your key but you, there is no way for this to be fraudulently manipulated unless you intentionally give your key to someone else.

This also means, however, that if you send your money to a scammer or if somehow a hacker steals them from your computer that there is no way to reverse it and get your funds back. So, while it can protect merchants, it can also create an issue. There are a few security methods you can take to prevent this from happening, however. They include storing your funds in an offline wallet on your computer and validating every merchant or individual that you send funds to.

Pseudonymous. Your transactions and your accounts that hold your funds are not connected to your identity when it comes to cryptocurrencies. For that reason, no one can connect you to your specific transactions. Even though they can see that the transaction has taken place, they cannot identify that it was *you* who made it. They also cannot identify who the secondary person was in your transaction. The identities of those involved in the transactions are completely anonymous.

In modern transactions, identities are tied to all transactions. This means that banks and other individuals can monitor your transaction activities and see what you are doing. When it comes to a security feature, this is an incredibly valid and valuable feature to have. It is easy to quickly identify who the scammers are, who is committing fraud, and issue penalties where they belong, rather than the victim being forced to pay the price. However, it can also mean that individuals outside of authorities and law enforcement can see your transactions. While not everyone cares about this, some people may prefer to have their transactions kept private. For this reason, having your keys completely anonymous may be a benefit.

Fast and Global. When you conduct a transaction with cryptocurrency, the transaction is typically very fast. Depending on what payment network you are using, you can also request to pay a small fee to have your transaction moved into a higher-priority level so that it is processed even faster. This means that you can quickly transfer funds around, no matter how large they are. From a few dollars to a few hundred thousand dollars, you can send them with minimal effort. And, since the entire network is built on a global level, you can transact these currencies to virtually anywhere in the world with no fees outside of those which you choose to pay should you want to increase the priority level of your transaction. That means if you want to send hundreds of thousands of dollars across borders for a business transaction, it can be done so instantaneously and without paying any fees to convert currencies or send them across borders.

This is an incredibly valuable feature as it means the cost of doing business becomes much more feasible for many, including startup companies. It also means that business can be conducted in a much shorter time frame as there are not several processes that need to be done and validated by banks before the transaction can be validated and considered "official" and complete.

Secure. Because of the decentralized system that cryptocurrencies are built on and the cryptography system used to create and transact them, cryptocurrencies are considered to be an incredibly secure form of currency. Short of you paying a scammer directly or someone hacking into your computer and stealing them, there are very few ways that your currencies can be fraudulently dealt with. It is virtually impossible to have people conduct fraudulent transactions with your currency, and once they are sent, they are gone. This means that there is no potential for the transaction to be interrupted, stolen, or otherwise affected or impacted in the transactional process. Cryptocurrencies are built with personal keys, and these keys are extremely secure. It is nearly impossible for anyone to break into them and begin using your account against your permission. So, unlike a bank account which can be fraudulently hacked and then have funds stolen from it, your cryptocurrency account cannot be hacked. It is completely secure to you and your key.

Permissionless. One of the biggest things about currency in the traditional form is that you have to get your funds converted and that in some cases you need some form of permission to get your funds. Since governments control the funds, they can prevent and bar you from using or trading in their regional currency. Cryptocurrency is not like that, however. Instead, it is a software that can be downloaded for free. Then, you can immediately begin receiving and sending cryptocurrencies. There are no government or authority figures involved, so there are nothing and no one to prevent you from using the currency at your own free will.

Is There a Future in Cryptocurrency?

Based on the excitement and popularity around cryptocurrency, we can conclude that it is not going anywhere. At least not in the near future. Not only are people eager to purchase and use it as it is, but the idea of what cryptocurrency could mean for our future and how we live our lives is also incredible.

People speculate and dream that one day we will have a world whereby all of our devices and personal belongings are equipped with their own "keys" which can automatically perform payments for us. For example, if you are low on food you would tell your fridge to purchase more groceries for you based on a preset list you have chosen, and it would use cryptocurrency and its unique cryptocurrency key, which would be linked to your wallet, to complete the transaction. They also hope that this will be possible for cars when it comes to charging them, and other similar features.

In essence, cryptocurrency is believed to be a way for us to bring a futuristic sci-fi type of world into our reality sooner than any of us may have originally expected. Although all of these features could easily be done with traditional currencies, the idea that we could use cryptocurrencies and bypass all of the banks and be the sole dealers and accountants of our own funds is fascinating. Not only would they be globally recognized, therefore making banks and other traditional financial institutions obsolete, but they would also be free of any traditional fees that we presently recognize. This means that you would be able to effortlessly process transactions anywhere, at any time, with little to no restrictions.

If you wanted to transfer money to family in a different country, it would cost significantly less meaning they would get to keep more of the money. If you wanted to purchase something from overseas, the transaction would clear in record timing and allow for you to complete the purchase much quicker than is presently possible. If you wanted to run a global empire, your business could operate seamlessly with no need to worry about currency conversions and other traditional currency-related issues that sometimes pose a difficulty or time-consuming manner in the modern era.

Why Should I Invest in Cryptocurrency Now?

There are many reasons why people are already getting started in investing in cryptocurrencies even though we are not entirely sure of the role they will have in our world in the future. While we can speculate, there are no guarantees on what will or will not happen with these currencies. However, it has been concluded that they are here to stay and that one way or another they are going to have some form of impact on the world.

Currently, many people are purchasing cryptocurrencies as a means to hedge themselves against the ever-fluctuating value of their national currencies. As their own national currencies devalue, owning and trading in cryptocurrencies can be more productive. They tend to have a more stable value long-term, and they seem to be on the uptrend more often than not. Some have even reached as high as $12,000USD+ value per coin!

With the ever-rising value of these coins and the ever-fluctuating state of the economy, investing now is better than waiting too long. With how rapidly the technology around cryptocurrencies is evolving and developing, getting involved sooner rather than later is the best way to ensure that you get on board and maximize the income you earn as a result of your investments. Whether you want to purchase them now and hold onto them until they potentially become usable on a wide-scale, or if you want to purchase them and sell them in a trading strategy to increase your funds, they are a great asset to invest in. They can help you diversify your portfolio and effectively embrace the future as it rapidly speeds towards us in the present.

Chapter 2: Choosing A Cryptocurrency

There are many different types of cryptocurrencies that have sprung about since the release of Bitcoin in 2009. As a result, there has been a wide amount of speculation as to which currency is the best to invest in and where you should be putting your attention. Many of these coins are viable competitors to Bitcoin, with some even being considered better or more advanced in their abilities and potential. Others seem to exist on a much smaller scale and may or may not provide the same value or benefits that larger coins might.

When you get started in investing in cryptocurrency, you want to make sure that you are investing in the right currency. You want to make sure that you pick one that is going to suit what you are looking for in regards to investment purposes, as well as one that you can rely on and ideally earn a profit from if you are in the business of trading.

To help you learn more about each coin that is presently available, where it currently sits in the marketplace, and why you might consider investing in it, we are going to explore the most popular and well-known coins that have become available in the cryptocurrency market.

Bitcoin

Topping our list of currencies is Bitcoin. This coin is the most popular coin because of how famous it has become as a result of being a pioneer in the modern cryptocurrency world. It was the first to launch, and it has topped the charts ever since. Despite other coins coming out, Bitcoin has remained at the top of the popularity ranking since its launch in 2009. Despite its popularity, however, there are other cryptocurrencies that are rapidly encroaching on its territory in the way of them being valid competitors in the marketplace.

Bitcoin is said to be like a digital version of gold. It has been used globally for payment methods, and many different online and even offline merchants have begun accepting this currency as a form of payment for goods and services. When people discuss cryptocurrencies, Bitcoins are typically the first thing that comes to mind. These coins began at a value of $0 and were originally launched as a beta program. Developers wanted to try and see if they could find a valid cryptocurrency format that would work, and it's safe to say that they did. Not only is Bitcoin still in existence today and rapidly growing in popularity, with it rapidly approaching $13,000 USD in value, but also holds the title as the pioneer for modern cryptocurrency technology. It is safe to say that they certainly mastered the algorithm and successfully designed a cryptocurrency that is valid and useful when they launched Bitcoin!

Ethereum

Since its launch in 2015, Ethereum has rapidly become second-in-place for the best cryptocurrency to get involved in. Despite being second in the cryptocurrency hierarchy, however, Ethereum has an incredible addition that Bitcoin does not have. That is, Ethereum has been designed to not only perform basic transactions but also to perform complex contracts and programs. It does so by using the Blockchain technology that was introduced upon the creation of Bitcoin.

Ethereum smart contracts and programs are essentially complex contracts that are created to determine how and when money will be issued. Once certain conditions are met, money will be released to the appropriate party. If, however, these conditions are never met, the money is never released.

The interesting thing about Ethereum is that it is actually created to be more of a family or set of cryptocurrencies versus a single cryptocurrency like Bitcoin. This means that Ethereum hosts several "tokens" which are used as a currency form. Some include DigixDAO and Augur. These tokens are then used to complete payments and transfer funds. Each unique token carries a different value. It is quite similar to how you may carry coins in your own physical wallet. Some might be worth just $0.10 whereas others are worth $1 or $2. When you invest in Ethereum, it pays to invest in several different tokens to further diversify your portfolio and maximize your potential gains.

Ripple

It is important that we talk about Ripple despite it being considered one of the least popular cryptocurrencies on the market. You do not want to get involved with something without fully understanding it, and since Ripple is widely talked about, it is important that you are completely aware of what you are getting into if you begin exploring Ripple as a cryptocurrency investment option.

Ripple is a form of cryptocurrency that is less than a

currency format and more of a debt format. The native cryptocurrency for this program is XRP, and it is not actually used as a medium to store and exchange value. Instead, it is used as a token to protect the network itself against spam.

Most people consider Ripple to be a poor investment and do not think it will last long or be worth it in the long run. Many cryptocurrency buffs call it a pre-mined software and believe it is not a real cryptocurrency but rather a network. However, the banks appear to really like Ripple and have begun adopting the system at an increasing pace.

Litecoin

Whereas Bitcoin is considered to be digital gold in the cryptocurrency world, Litecoin is considered to be digital silver. This coin quickly launched just after Bitcoin, making it the second cryptocurrency to truly emerge on the scene of modern cryptocurrencies.

When they developed Litecoin, it is believed that they developed it as a "2.0" version of Bitcoin. They made it so that the transactions and mining process are faster than in Bitcoin technology, and also so that there are more tokens, as well as new mining algorithms.

This cryptocurrency was perfectly designed to be the smaller and more readily available version of Bitcoin. Whereas Bitcoin may hold higher marketplace value and popularity, Litecoin tends to be much easier for people to get started with and use in investments and trading.

The biggest setback with Litecoin is that people preferred to use Bitcoin over Litecoin and therefore no one ever found a real use for it. For that reason, people stopped using it widely and instead favored Bitcoin. However, the coin is still mined and traded, and many people hoard it just in case Bitcoin ever fails.

Monero

After Bitcoin was created, developers realized there were further ways that security could be enhanced and the algorithms could be stronger. As a result, they developed the CryptoNight algorithm and launched Monero. The biggest example of how these two differ is with the blockchain transactions. Bitcoin is hashed on the blockchain, and a trail of transactions follows it, always. There is no way to cut through this. With Monero, however, you can cut through them.

The first time that the CryptoNight algorithm was introduced was in a coin known as Bytecoin, and it was highly rejected by the cryptocurrency community. This was because the cryptocurrency was heavily premined. However, they managed to later launch Monero which is the first time they ever launched the CryptoNight algorithm as a non-premined clone of the original Bytecoin. Although many others have since emerged, Monero has maintained its position as the most popular variation of a cryptocurrency existing with CryptoNight algorithms.

Monero has continued to steadily increase in pricing, however the ways it can be used remains extremely small. For that reason, it may be worth investing in, but many people are losing faith that it will have any form of significant future in the economy or marketplace. Rather than being a good investment as a currency itself, the technology is a better investment as it provides a form of playground for the developers to build on.

Making an Investment Choice

Choosing which coin to invest in really depends on what you are looking for. If you want to have a basic coin that you can invest in and trade, Bitcoin is likely the best way for you to go. This cryptocurrency revolves around a single form of token and is the most popular, which is likely the very reason why the price has continued to steadily increase for nearly a decade since the technology was launched.

The next best form of currency to get into is Ethereum. This currency is rapidly sidling up to Bitcoin as the best cryptocurrency technology and easily takes second place as most popular. While Ethereum is more of a family of tokens versus a single kind, it is still a great cryptocurrency to invest in. If you choose to invest in Ethereum, make sure you choose one of the more popular token to invest in, such as the DigixDAO or Augur. Do your research before investing in any particular token so that you are not investing in something that will not earn you a strong return.

If you want to consider a less-expensive and still fairly valuable coin to invest in, Litecoin is a great place to start. While you will not make nearly as much return as you will with Bitcoin or Ethereum, it is a much lower buy-in and can be a great way to diversify your cryptocurrency investment profile and also protect yourself should Bitcoin ever fail.

If you are considering investing in something different that is considered to be more of a playground or a test program, Monero may be the way to go. While you likely will not get a strong return on this coin, you will be on the trail of a new form of an algorithm that has emerged in the cryptocurrency world. This means that if anything ever changes and goes strongly in Monero's favor, you will already be on board.

Avoid investing in Ripple at all costs. There is very little to be said about this program other than the fact that it is not widely accepted, not an advancement on technology, and will likely not go anywhere. You will not make a strong return on your investment and will likely find yourself out a lot of money if you trail this cryptocurrency and try to earn any form of return on it.

Making the Choice for Purchasing

If you are looking to get into a currency that you can both invest in and purchase products with, Bitcoin and Ethereum remain the two best choices. Both of these have a wide and ever-growing range of uses and are being accepted by more and more merchants all of the time. Not only are you likely to make a great return on your investment, but you can also actively use them for shopping and transactions to get an idea of what purchasing things with cryptocurrency is truly like.

The other forms of cryptocurrency have a very small backing in the marketplace which means that there are few things you can actually purchase with them. While they may be okay for trading and investing, or diversifying your investments portfolio, they are not ideal when it comes to shopping of any sort.

Chapter 3: Buying and Storing Cryptocurrencies

After you have chosen the type of cryptocurrency or cryptocurrencies you want to begin investing in, you can go ahead and start the process of buying and storing them. In this chapter, we will discuss how these two parts of the process work and what you need to do to get started yourself.

How Does Buying Work?

Buying cryptocurrencies can be fun and easy and has the potential to help you earn a great return if you get involved in it in regards to trading. However, you have to first know how to actually buy your tokens or coins before you can begin doing anything with them.

Buying any cryptocurrencies is different from getting other forms of currency. You are not simply compensated for something and then head to the bank to cash in or switch it to a different currency if you want to make money through another means. Instead, you have to use digital platforms to buy your coins.

There are many platforms available for purchasing cryptocurrencies on. In general, they work fairly simply: find a platform, create an account, and begin. However, you need to make sure that you are using the best platform to get started. Some platforms are less secure, go offline frequently, or may not have access to the types of coins you want to invest in. So, be sure to research the specific platform that you want to use before you get started. A great place to start if you are looking to trade in any of the cryptocurrencies mentioned in the previous chapter of this book is Coinbase. In the next section where we talk about buying your first tokens, we will talk about Coinbase specifically.

Using a more well-known and popular purchasing platform means that you have more secured transactions and that the platform remains online more. Some may go offline regularly which can make buying and trading in cryptocurrencies annoying and frustrating. There are also a lot less glitches and kinks with more well-known applications.

Once you have chosen an application, it is as simple as making an account and getting started. On your platform, you will see that you have the opportunity to purchase and sell your coins. You will find more information and tips regarding what to do in the buying and selling process in Chapter 4, but ultimately that is the gist of it. It truly is one of the simplest investments to get started on. The biggest part of the process is research, the investment process itself takes minimal timing.

Buying Your First Coins

Now that you know how easy it is to get started, it's time to learn how you can buy your first tokens! As previously mentioned, this process is outlined using the Coinbase application or network, which is currently the most widely used one. However, any network you choose to use will work in the same general manner.

With Coinbase, you want to start by either downloading the

application on your phone or visiting the Coinbase website. There, you will find a "sign up" button that allows you to begin creating your account. You will need to input some basic personal information, including your name, e-mail and chosen password. Then, you will need to go ahead and confirm that you agree to the terms and conditions of the website. Once you have done so, they will e-mail you a verification e-mail. You will need to open that e-mail and click the link to confirm your account.

With your account completely verified and ready to go, it is time to start buying coins! This part of the process is extremely simple. Go to either the application or website and login with your new account information. Then, add a way to purchase. This is typically by linking your bank account to the application. Once you have, you can simply tap the "Buy" button on the app, or the "Buy/Sell" tab on the website. Hit the buy button once more and then determine which type of currency you want to buy and how much US dollars you want to spend to purchase that currency. Next, it will tell you how much of the currency you are buying. Confirm the transaction, and you are done!

There are other cryptocurrency exchanges that are up-and-coming and popular among the cryptocurrency world. If you are looking for the opportunity to begin purchasing and selling and do not want to use Coinbase, other contenders include Kraken, Poloniex, Bittrex, Binance, Bitfinex, Bithumb, Shapeshift, Kucoin, Cobinhood, Coinone, CEX.IO, and Coinsquare.io.

How Does Storing Work?

Storing your cryptocurrencies requires you to have a cryptocurrency wallet. It is imperative that you store your coins properly to prevent yourself from losing them or having them stolen. While many networks, such as Coinbase, will provide you with a wallet, keeping them somewhere slightly more secure is a good idea.

When it comes to storing cryptocurrencies, there are two types of wallets. They are hot wallets and cold wallets. A hot wallet is stored online and is subjected to more risks and potential threats than a cold wallet, which is stored offline. Cold wallets are not connected to the internet which makes them a lot harder for anyone to hack into and steal your funds. If you are going to be storing or trading fairly large amounts, it is a good idea to store the bulk of your funds in a cold wallet and only store what you are actively going to use in a hot wallet.

Your wallet has a private key, and it is mandatory that you give this key to *no one*, not even your spouse or anyone that you trust. This means that you should also refrain from using wallets that are based on major exchange networks because the keys are stored on their servers which can make them easier to access if someone were to hack the servers. Ideally, this would never happen, but you can never be to safe when your funds are involved! To really ensure that you protect yourself, you want to make sure that you always store the bulk of your funds in a cold wallet, as previously mentioned. Only store them in a hot wallet if you are actively trading or using them. That way if your hot wallet ever gets hacked, the substantial portion of your funds are protected offline.

Hot wallets are available by downloading applications or using computer websites that work to store cryptocurrencies. Some of the most popular ones include Coinbase (only what you are going to be exchanging right away or in the very near future), Blockchain.info, Electrum, and Ledger or Trezor.

Cold wallets work differently. They require you to do what is called a paper wallet, where you essentially download a document that contains all of the information you need to generate the private keys that you need to access your coins. Generally, this exists on a piece of paper that has a QR code that you can scan into a software wallet when you want to access them. When you store your cryptocurrencies offline like this, it makes them significantly safer against hacking and fraud. However, you can also store them offline on a USB drive or other external media, on a bearer item such as those known as "physical bitcoins," or even on an offline hardware wallet available for cryptocurrency traders.

This may seem confusing, but once you get the hang of it, it becomes easier for you to understand. In the following section, we will discuss exactly how you can store your coins.

Storing Your New Coins

There are two methods of storage we are going to discuss: hot wallets and cold wallets. As previously mentioned, you want to store the majority of, if not all of, your coins in your cold wallet. The only coins you need to save in your hot wallet are those that you plan on using or trading in the near future. We are going to start by discussing your hot wallet as this is where your newly purchased coins will be transferred into.

If you are using Coinbase, you will have your coins automatically transferred into your Coinbase wallet. However, you may choose to use an alternative wallet or create a new wallet if you are using a different exchange. The easiest way to generate an online wallet is to go to Bitcoin.org if you are choosing to exchange in Bitcoin, and Jaxx or Electrum. These are software-based wallets that are considered hot wallets because they store your coins online on a mobile platform. To create a wallet with these platforms, simply visit their websites and follow the steps to create your own wallet. They will outline them for you, making the process extremely simple.

Now, when it comes to doing a cold wallet, it takes a bit longer. This depends on what type of cold wallet you intend on creating. Below we have outlined the steps for making a paper wallet. These are the easiest form of offline wallets you can create that will protect your investment and keep your funds safe. As long as you do not lose the paper, you are completely fine. You should store the paper in a safe place where it will not become damaged, and then you can easily access your funds at any time that you need them. This guide is for Bitcoin, but you can do the same for any cryptocurrency by accessing the native website and following similar steps. Here's how.

First, you want to go to the Bitcoin.com website and access the paper wallet tool. There, you want to press Ctrl-S to save the page locally to your computer. You also want to make sure that you create an offline address when you are there. Then, close out of the webpage and disconnect your computer from the internet. This will only be for a few minutes until you are done creating your paper wallet, then you can reconnect it.

After it is disconnected, open the save file of the website you just saved locally. Once you have, you want to move your mouse around and then tap some random keys on your keyboard a few times. This causes it to create a random Bitcoin address that will be equipped with both a public and private key-pair. This address will have been created completely offline since you disconnected from the internet when you were creating it.

Once you have created your key, print the page. You want to do this while the computer is still disconnected from the internet. To print the page, you want to make sure that your printer is also offline and manually connected to your computer. You do not want to have any of your devices connected to the internet during this process as this can compromise your key-pair.

With your page now printed in this manner, you have a completely offline set of public and private keys that are not documented online. The page you have will be equipped with a QR code for your private key and a visible copy of your public key. Keep this somewhere secure, such as in a fireproof safe to prevent it from becoming damaged or destroyed under any circumstances.

Once you have completely printed this off and you are done, you can reconnect your device to the internet and begin using your computer as normal once more. Never share your private key with anyone, regardless of this is online or offline. Sharing it could result in you losing your funds which would be devastating and disappointing.

If you want to add money to this wallet, you simply want to scan the public QR code and place it into the exchange where you would be "sending funds." This can be done on any popular cryptocurrency exchange network.

To redeem the coins, simply use a hot wallet that supports private keys and scan the QR code or use the private key address. Then, you will be able to access and redeem any of the funds you have in the wallet.

To Summarize

Getting started with cryptocurrency trading is not as hard as it may sound. In fact, it is pretty simple once you understand it. The biggest key is determining which currency you want to invest in, and then learning how you can purchase, spend, and store your coins. It is important that you use a trusted network when purchasing and selling your coins to refrain from being scammed. Even though the network itself is typically safe, there are many instances where untrustworthy people may get involved in deals with you and then take your coins without returning funds as promised. As well, even though it's not common on the major exchange networks, they can be hacked which can compromise your private information. It is important that you choose one that is verified as safe and that is not known to have any fraudulent activity taking place on it at any given time. You can easily do some online research about the network you want to use before you commit to ensure that you are using a safe one that will not result in you having any negative experiences with your investing and trading.

Once you have opened your account, buying is extremely simple. Most of the major exchange networks will walk you through the process step-by-step. They also have built-in wallets. They will also guide you toward other recommended wallets to store your cash. Remember, these are called hot wallets for a reason. That is because they are somewhat unsafe. You should never store a large amount of your coins in these wallets. Instead, store them safely in an offline manner such as with a paper wallet. Then, when you need to access them, transfer them to your hot wallet. The only coins you should have access to from your hot wallet are ones that you are going to use in the immediate or very near future. If there is going to be any gap of time between when you receive them and when you plan on using them, you should move them to your cold wallet. It only takes a few minutes, and it can truly save you from having a potentially devastating experience of losing your coins to some form of fraudulent activity, such as a hack. Even hot wallets that are considered to be the most secure are not completely free of risk, so you want to do your best to protect your investment and be smart about your storage solutions.

Once you have stored your funds, you can easily transfer them back into your hot wallet to be used at any time. Simply put them into the hot wallet and sell them to receive your native or desired currency, or you can spend them with merchants who accept the form of cryptocurrency that you have available to shop with.

It may seem extremely confusing at first, especially when you first see all of the screens associated with the exchanges, trading, hot wallets, and cold wallets. However, once you get the hang of it by trying it out a time or two, it becomes significantly easier. Soon, you will be buying, selling, trading, and spending cryptocurrencies as effortlessly as you presently do with your traditional currency.

Chapter 4: Tips for Mastering Cryptocurrency Investing and Trading

To make sure you get the most of your experience and truly master the art of trading with cryptocurrency, we are going to discuss some tips that you can use to master the art of cryptocurrency investing and trading. Using these tips will ensure that you do not make any fatal beginner mistakes and that you protect your assets and maximize the returns you get from your investments.

It is a good idea to review these tips *before* you begin investing to ensure that you know as much as you can before you get started. Although it is a fairly simple concept and you can get started relatively easily, it is important that you know as much as you can before you invest any of your cash into these currencies. If you do it right, you are likely to make a great return. Plus, it is always proper investment etiquette to make sure that you effectively research any investment before you actually invest in it. That way you don't make any uneducated decisions that could result in you losing out on cash!

Buy with Funds You Don't Need

Especially when you are getting started, you should only invest with funds that you do not need. If you think you may be able to invest in a cryptocurrency with money that you actually need so that you can double it and get-rich-quick, think again. Investments, especially in cryptocurrencies, are something that takes time to accumulate and build money. While you may get lucky and make a couple of hundred dollars, or even a couple of thousand dollars, in a relatively short period of time, you should not expect that this will happen. Generally, when you invest in cryptocurrencies, you should expect your investment to stay put for a fairly lengthy amount of time. The longer you leave your investment, the better your return on it will be. For that reason, you only want to use money that you don't need.

In addition to giving you a greater chance to earn more, it also saves you from a potential financial ruin if you invest money that you didn't have to begin with. If you were to invest it and something went wrong in your investment, and you lost all of your funds, or if the market crashed and the value of the currency went out the window, you want to make sure that you didn't have a lot riding on that investment. A general rule of thumb when investing in something as volatile and unpredictable as cryptocurrency is that you never want to invest with money that you expect you will need. Instead, invest and hope for the best, but prepare for the worst. If you come out on top with a healthy return on your investment, that's great! Ideal, even. However, if you end up coming out on the bottom, you want to be sure that the money you had tied up in your investments wasn't essential to your overall wellbeing. This is not only true with cryptocurrency investments but any investment in general.

A good way to start is to take a small amount of money and invest it. Many people like to start with just $50-$100. Then, they invest it and play around with it to see how it works. Learn what to watch for in the marketplace, how to buy, and when to sell. Once you get the hang of it with a smaller amount, you can begin putting more and more funds into it whenever you desire. You may choose to put a set amount each check into the investment, or you may simply put extra funds in any time you have them. Either way, make sure it's extra money and not money you need. Even if you seem to have "mastered" it, you should know that there is always a chance that it could go south, fast. This is not to scare you from investing at all, only to warn you against investing poorly.

Research First, Buy and Trade Second

It is imperative that you research cryptocurrency before you buy into it. You are off to a great start by reading this book. Now, you have a strong idea of what the most popular forms of cryptocurrency are, how you can acquire them, how you can store them, and how you can trade or use them. That is important. However, you should not let it stop here.

When you are investing in anything, including cryptocurrencies, it is important that you invest in them *after* you have researched them. You do not want to find yourself investing in something that you don't fully understand, only to lose your investment because you were not clear on what you were doing. It is important that you spend time researching the exchange network you are going to use, the cryptocurrency form that you want to invest in, and the recent and historical market figures for that particular coin.

A great way to research cryptocurrency comes from basic internet searches, but you should go deeper than that, too, if you want to make a really informed decision. There are many cryptocurrency forums and groups online that you can get into that will connect you with people who have already been trading in cryptocurrencies for quite some time. Getting involved in these forums gives you the opportunity to communicate with other traders and find out what is the best move for you to make at your beginner stage. The market is constantly changing, and so are the available currencies. For this reason, anything we may be able to recommend to you right now in this book may quickly become invalid. That is why we have not recommended any one specific coin for you to get started with but rather educated you on the most popular coins at the time of writing this book.

In addition to researching before you trade the first time, make sure you continue to research before every major trade and throughout the duration of your investments. As we just discussed, the market is constantly changing, and so are the range of available cryptocurrencies. It could change at any given time with the introduction of a new technology or cryptocurrency, so you want to make sure that you stay on top of it and pay attention. The more you research first, the more likely you will make wise, educated investment decisions. This can protect you against uneducated decisions that could cost you in the long run, and helps you get more out of your investments.

Diversify Only If You Understand

To expand on the importance of researching first, make sure that you only diversify when you understand what you are diversifying for, and what you are diversifying into. Some people suggest that you buy a small amount of every cryptocurrency currently available. This is actually a really poor investment choice. Some you can already clearly tell are not going to be very much, and if you were to do some research, you would know that. Some are simply experiments to learn about new technology and see what can be done with cryptocurrency. Others are revealed as an opportunity for new developers to get in on the cryptocurrency buzz and are not actually developed that well at all, making them virtually useless to you. There is no sense wasting any of your funds in these types of cryptocurrencies when you could simply research them and invest in ones that are more likely to succeed.

Furthermore, do not look to diversify your portfolio right away. Start with one cryptocurrency that you have already researched and spend some time getting to know how to use the cryptocurrency, how to navigate the exchange, and how to use your wallet storages. Once you have gotten comfortable with that cryptocurrency, look at alternative solutions of what you can buy into, and then buy into them once you are ready. Never buy into a currency that you don't understand, or into a wide series of cryptocurrencies without any clear understanding of why you are investing in them. You don't want to waste any of your assets investing in things that are going nowhere. You can find this out simply by researching them. Always research first, buy second. This includes when it comes to diversifying out into alternative coins.

Pay Attention to the Market Cap
You Don't Have to Buy a Whole Coin

Many people falsely believe that if you cannot afford to buy an entire coin, there is no sense getting involved in the market. That is completely false. If you want to get into Bitcoin or any other expensive cryptocurrency, you can do so with whatever funds you have available to you. This may seem confusing, especially since with traditional currency we couldn't possibly dream of owning a portion of a coin and it being worth anything, but in cryptocurrency terms, it makes complete sense.

When you own a percentage of a coin, then realistically other people would combine to own the other percentage of the same coin. When you choose to sell your percentage, you will make back that percentage of the coin.

To make it sound less confusing, let's look at a basic example.

Say a coin is worth $1,000 and you invest $100 in the coin. You then own 10% of that coin. If the coin value increases to $10,000, then your 10% of the share would increase to $1,000. Because it is a digital asset, you can easily own a share of a coin, versus the entire coin itself. Do not feel as though you cannot invest in a coin simply because you do not currently have the market value of the coin. For example, when bitcoin reaches $13,000, you do not need $13,000 to buy the coin. Instead, buy a portion of it with the funds you do have. Cryptocurrency exchanges allow you to choose how much of your native currency you want to invest in the coin, and then they give you that respective percentage of the coin. Even if you only own 0.002% of the coin, which is a considerably small portion it seems, you can still make a significant return if the market goes up 20%.

Do not worry about how much of the coin you can buy, simply worry about investing in the one that suits your needs. If you want to invest $50 in a $13,000 coin, you can still make a fair return on that. There is nothing that states that you cannot do this. Do not be afraid of this number; you can still safely invest in these coins in most cases.

Unless Circumstances Change, Don't Take Profits

Many people feel that you should take the profits of your funds out right away. Of course, this is entirely up to you. Most people will say that you should go ahead and quickly sell so that you can collect a massive profit. If that is what works for you and that is what you are looking for, then, by all means, do that.

However, ideally, there are only a few things that would result in you really needing to remove your funds. For example, if your income changes and you really need the funds, you could sell them and take your profits. Or, if you choose that you want to remove your funds and invest elsewhere. You may also choose to remove your initial investment for peace of mind so that you know for sure that no matter what happens, you are not going to lose your original investment.

Of course, you may have other personal reasons for wanting to remove your profits that may be entirely up to you. If you really need them, if you want to go on a vacation, or really anything else. It *is* your funds, so it is entirely up to you what you choose to do with them.

However, it is worth noting that the longer they sit, the bigger they grow. Rather than dipping into them, unless absolutely necessary, it may be a better idea to leave them alone and let them continue to accumulate so that one day when you do actually need them, they are available to you.

Cryptocurrency is Not for Day Traders

Many modern traders have a tendency to skim the market on a daily basis. They enter in the morning with low buy-ins and sell in the evening with high payouts. This is completely fine in many market places, but it is not a valuable practice in cryptocurrency. When it comes to cryptocurrency, you want to let it sit and accumulate for as long as possible. Rapidly buying and selling your funds can result in you losing out on valuable growth.

If you want to invest in cryptocurrency, you should look to it as a long-term investment instead of something that you can get in and out of in a relatively short period of time. While some people choose to take the profits and make massive returns in a short period of time, the real prize is in letting it sit and accumulate. The longer it sits, the bigger it grows. It is not unheard of for people to buy in with $1,000 and walk out with $80,000.

For this same reason, do not worry about being right on every single trade. You are going to make mistakes that will result in you not getting the maximum return on your investment. This is especially the case if you are new and if you do not have any substantial experience with investments. Instead of trying to be right every single time and making minimal investments, seek to be right when it really counts and make the most of your investments that you can. The goal is to make as much money as possible, so seek to do that and don't worry about mistakes you make along the way. You will learn and do better for the most part. But also, not every mistake can be completely avoided. Even the most advanced and avid traders in virtually every market make massive mistakes on a fairly consistent basis. A good trader, however, will know how to make decisions following that which will bring them back into the green.

Buy Low, Sell High, And...

When it comes to buying low and selling high, this is virtually always true in no matter what market you are trading in. So, naturally, it counts for cryptocurrencies as well. Because of how volatile the cryptocurrency market can be, however, this may not always be easy. It is hard to predict where the peaks and valleys are going to lie with cryptocurrencies as they can often take massive and seemingly irrational turns one way or another at any given time.

Instead of worrying so much about buying low and selling high, focus on buying low, holding onto the coins as long as you can, and then selling when they're high. You may not be able to predict the peaks due to the volatility of the market, so you want to make sure that you are focused on the long-term gains, not the short-term ones. Trying to predict the market in a short period of time can get stressful and result in you losing out on potentially major gains. Instead, look at the bigger picture and pay attention to it overall. Look beyond 24-hour spans and into weeks, or even months and years. This makes it much easier to determine where the general market is going and what moves you should make as a result.

Buy Now

Many people are worried about when to buy into the market. They are unsure about when they should buy in, they don't know if it is the right time, and they want to make sure that they get the most back. This is completely normal and natural. Obviously, this is likely why you are investing in cryptocurrency: to make a return. However, there is no optimal buy-in time. The longer you wait, the higher the price goes, and the higher your buy-in price will be.

Do not wait for the right time or try and predict when a valley will come so that you can buy in. Instead, buy in right now. Buy only what you can afford, get started with that, and then focus on buying *more* once it hits a low point. That makes it much easier for you to actually get started and not feel quite so intimidated in the world of cryptocurrency. For the first week or two, make it about learning and getting used to the market. Then, once you have, you can start paying attention to pulling the right moves and getting your low buy-ins and high payouts.

The only really bad move you can make when it comes to buying into a cryptocurrency is waiting so long that you become intimidated by the idea, or not completely researching the currency you choose to buy into before you actually buy into it. Take enough time to research, and then pull the trigger. If you start with a relatively small amount, like $100 or less, then it won't hurt so much if you make mistakes in the learning process. Keeping the pressure off in the beginning while you learn to understand it can make the entire process a lot easier.

Buy the Rumor, Sell the News

There is a phrase in trading that goes "buy the rumor, sell the news." This essentially means that you want to listen to what rumors are saying and, if many are in agreeance, buy in. For example, if there are rumors that a certain coin is going to rapidly increase in value, buy in! Then, if and when it actually does increase, you will be the one selling the news, not reading it or listening to it.

Although this can sometimes result in you not always making the best trades or losing out, it also puts you in the running to stand for a lot of gains. Since the entire idea is to earn as many funds as you possibly can, the more you stand to win, the better. Of course, you do not want to make an uneducated decision, so make sure that the rumors you are listening to are coming from reputable sources. Pay attention to other traders, media surrounding trades and investments, and other similar sources. As long as the rumor comes from a credible source and there are many people spreading the rumor, there is a good chance that it could come true. If you are worried about it not coming true, however, you can always invest a smaller amount.

Practice and Get Comfortable

The ultimate goal when it comes to trading and investing in cryptocurrencies is that you take your time, practice, and get comfortable. If you practice with funds that were not necessary and that you won't be overly upset over if you lose them, then any mistakes you make early on will not be as upsetting.

Getting started in anything new, especially trades and investments, can be confusing. Early on, you are learning to navigate new software, store your coins, and understand the market. Give yourself some time and some practice money to figure it all out, and then once it begins to make sense to you, you can start investing more into it. The more you learn to navigate the software, get used to transferring your funds and storing them, and knowing when to buy and when to sell your coins, the easier it becomes. As well, this will give you time to learn how to be patient and accumulate overall market gains, rather than getting antsy and buying and selling too frequently. Once you get used to the entire process, it will be easy for you and you will likely find that you can create incredible returns with this form of investment and trading.

Conclusion

Cryptocurrency is the way of the future, there is no doubt about it. Whether it is only going to be an addition to the existing currency, or if it will eventually replace it entirely, it pays to get on board and begin learning how cryptocurrencies work. Furthermore, there can be some pretty substantial profits made from investing in cryptocurrencies.

Getting started can be intimidating, especially if you have never been directly involved in investments or trades before. Unlike traditional currency whereby you can hire an investment portfolio manager to do the work for you, you are responsible for investing in and trading your own cryptocurrencies. Fortunately, there are many exchange networks you can use that make this process easy, even for beginners who have very little background knowledge on the trading side of finances.

I hope this book was able to help you understand more about how cryptocurrencies work, why they are so revolutionary, and what you need to do to begin trading them. Remember, this book is a beginner's guide, and it gives you phenomenal information to get started and actively buy, use, trade, and store cryptocurrencies. However, before you fully commit to any particular cryptocurrency, it is important that you take additional time to research that specific cryptocurrency. There are constantly new forms of cryptocurrencies emerging, and each one has unique traits, properties, and benefits. They also change rapidly, and so too can their popularity. If you want to make the best move, it is a good idea to investigate the specific coin you are most interested in before you commit to purchasing anything.

The next step is for you to determine which cryptocurrency best encompasses what you want to gain from cryptocurrency, and research it further. Then, when you are ready, you can create an account with a popular exchange network and create your hot wallet. Once everything is set up, you can go ahead and begin purchasing, selling, and trading currencies. Be sure that you start small so that any mistakes you may make early on as you are learning are not devastating to your overall finances. Only use funds that you do not need for any other reason.

Lastly, if you enjoyed this book, please take the time to honestly review it on Amazon Kindle. Your honest feedback would be greatly appreciated.

Thank you, and good luck!

www.ingramcontent.com/pod-product-compliance
Lightning Source LLC
Chambersburg PA
CBHW030639220526
45463CB00004B/1574